## HUNDREDS OF EXTRAORDINARY SIGHTS

Jeff Bahr

Publications International, Ltd.

## Picture Credits

Front cover: **Laurence Parent Photography**

Back cover: **Alamy Images/imagebroker**

**Accent Alaska:** 313; **age fotostock:** Heeb Christian, 217; **Alamy Images:** 89, 204; Jeffrey Blackler, 92; Jim Corwin, 274, 275; Chris A. Crumley, 114; Danita Delimont, 225; Franck Fotos, 108, 214, 280, 287; Jeff Greenberg, 9, 120, 121; imagebroker, 242–243, 267; INTERFOTO Pressebildagentur, 256; Andre Jenny, 115; LHB Photo, contents, 4, 5, 292, 293; Mervyn Rees, 265; Stephen Saks Photography, 290 (bottom); Kevin Taylor, 261; Visions of America, LLC, 173 (bottom), 302; Jim West, 85 (top); Phil Wills, 229 (bottom); **American Museum of Magic:** 141; **Eve Andersson:** 259; **AP Images:** 8, 14 (right), 20, 29 (bottom), 39, 68, 85 (bottom), 94, 110, 125, 162, 163, 172, 173 (top), 238 (bottom), 239, 264, 269, 286, 298; **Barker Character, Comic & Cartoon Museum,** 40–41; **Michael Bates:** 181 (bottom); **Gary W. Becker:** 64; **Walter Bibikow:** title page, contents, 48–49, 72, 73, 304; **Randa Bishop:** 255; **Bob Pardue Photography:** 191 (top); **Bobbi Lane Photography:** 154; **Bonnie@naturalbridgeva.com:** 187 (bottom); **Adam Bowling:** 155 (bottom left); **Larry Caine:** 127; **Cave City Tourism Bureau:** Howard Margolis, 90; **Churchill & Klehr:** 142; **Cockroach Hall of Fame:** 221; **Eliot Cohen & Judith Jango-Cohen:** 24, 25; **Coolstock.com:** Collection, 105, 271; © 2004 Saari, 195 (top);**© Corbis:** Tony Arruza, 123; Bettmann, 28, 119, 161 (bottom); Richard Cummins, 205; Deanne Fitzmaurice/San Francisco Chronicle, 290 (top); Stephen Frink, 116; David Kadlubowski, 118; Wolfgang Kaehler, 251; Catherine Karnow, 148; Layne Kennedy, 198; Charles & Josette Lenars, 233; James Marshall, 238 (top); Buddy Mays, 128 (top); John McAnulty, 305; Christopher Morris, 30 (right); Bob Rowan/Progressive Image, 235; Paul A. Souders, 301, 303; Ted Soqui, 215; **Craig Corbitt:** 117; **Creative Services:** Charles Plant, 104; **David Brownell Photography:** 33; **Grace Davies:** 19 (top); **Donald Davis:** 55; **Julie Demler:** 155 (top & bottom right); **Devil's Rope Barbed Wire Museum:** 220 (top); **Downtown Collinsville, Inc.:** Michael Gassmann, 150; **drr.net:** 74, 80, 279, 281, 285; Maria Aufmuth, 291; Julie Bennett, 308; Johnny Bivera, 70; Darlene Bordwell, 65; Carol Burkett/Superior Imaging, 248, 249; John J. Van Decker, 75; Erin Paul Donovan, 31; Steve Greene, 143; James F. Harrington, 36, 37; Isaac Hernandez, contents, 202–203, 208, 209; Kerrick James, 240 (left); Adam Jones/Danita Delimont Agency, 91 (bottom left & bottom right); Al Karevy, 18; Camille Nims Lamoureux, 224; G.R. Lindblade & Co., 174, 175, 190; Derek Rankins, 178, 179; Eric Reed, 278; Danielle Richards, 52, 53, 56, 57 (left), 71; David Sanger, 284; Philip Scalia, 58, 59, 60, 61; Randy Wells, 306; Nik Wheeler, 16, 17, 192, 193, 240 (right); Melissa Witteveen/Green Horizon Images, 309; **John Elk III:** 11 (bottom), 130, 188, 189, 219, 294, 297; **Enchanted Highway:** 199; **Enchilada Festival:** 211; **Eric Hatch Photography:** 134 (top); **Fair Haven Photographs:** Joanne Pearson, contents, 12, 46; **Fargo-Moorhead Convention and Visitors Bureau:** 201; **Ben Fink:** 95; **Maureen Blaney Flietner:** 158; **Flying Fish Photography:** Ron & Diane Salmon, 69, 82, 83, 100; **Joshua Friedman:** 86; **Getty Images:** 14 (left); Mario Tama, 126 (top); Time Life Pictures, 29 (top), 283; **Ron Gilbert:** 288, 289; **Glore Psychiatric Museum:** 176; **God's Ark of Safety:** 68; **Jeff Goldberg:** 137; **Graceland Too:** 126 (bottom left & bottom right); **Larry Harris:** 236, 237; **Rick Hebenstreit:** 253; **Henry's Rabbit Ranch:** 149; **Hippos Unlimited:** Mike Fowler, 226; **Homer & Langley's Mystery Spot:** Laura Levine, 62; **Casey Hopkins, DarkDestinations.com:** 128 (bottom); **Hot Topic Images:** Wendy White, 272–273, 300, 307, 310, 311; **The House on the Rock:** 156; **Houserstock:** Jan Butchofsky-Houser, 268; Dave G. Houser, 26 (right), 185, 195 (bottom), 234; **The Image Finders:** Betts Anderson, 165; Howard Andre, 263; Jim Baron, 136; Mark E. Gibson, 296; Bruce Leighy, 99; **The Image Works:** Mike Douglas, 168; Eastcott/Momatiuk, 197; Jeff Greenberg, 81, 129 (top); Teake Zuidema, 103; **ImageState:** 124; **Courtesy Isle of Wight County Museum:** 78 (bottom); **iStockphoto:** 112 (top); **Jack Olson Photography:** 152, 196, 245, 246, 257 (right), 312; **James P. Rowan Photography:** 27, 151, 167; **Jordan's Furniture Store and Trapeze School:** 21; **Jungle Jim's:** 138, 139; **Kim Karpeles:** 147; **James Kirkikis:** 42, 43, 107; **Knight's Spider Web Farm:** Michael Knight, 15; **Jacob Krejci:** 96; **John Lander:** 131; **Laurence Parent Photography:** 132–133, 186, 257 (left); **Leila's Hair Museum:** Leila Cahoon, 177; **Ronald Lessman:** 187 (top); **David Liebman:** 78 (top left & top right), 79; **Longhorn Grill:** 241; **Lost River Cave:** 88; **Lunchbox Museum:** 109; **McConnell & McNamara:** 45, 47; **Danton McDiffett:** 181 (top); **Chris McSorley:** 282; **Medioimages/Photodisc:** 314; **Michael Morton Photography:** Michael Morton, 222, 223; **Eugene C. Morris:** 122; **Mount Washington Valley Chamber of Commerce:** 32; **Museum of Bad Art:** 22, 23; **National Residential Wax Museum:** 191 (bottom); **New England Pest Control:** 38; **© N.Y.S. Department of Economic Development 2004:** 63; **Nichols Design:** D.B. Cooper, 250; **Nik Wheeler Photography:** 113, 210, 295; **North Dakota Tourism:** 200; **okienoodling.com:** 218; **Oklahoma Tourism:** Fred W. Marvel, 216; **Old Jail Museum, Jim Thorpe, PA:** 54 (right); Patricia Kane-Vanni, 54 (left); **Orange Show Center for Visionary Art:** Paul Hester, 228, 229 (top); **Hans Owens:** 270; **Palace of Gold:** 84; **Rhoda Peacher:** 276, 277; **Photo Researchers, Inc.:** Michael P. Gadomski, 51; Larry Landolfi, 30 (left); **PhotoEdit:** Jeff Greenberg, 10; **Photolibrary:** Mark Gibson, 87; **Photri, Inc.:** 50; B. Leighty, 266; **Powder Hill Photography LLC:** 161 (top); **QuadPhoto:** Zach Bowen, 13; **Murray Riss:** 95; **Robert Holmes Photography:** 307; **Greg Ryan/Sally Beyer:** 160, 166; **Debra Jane Seltzer:** 67, 134 (bottom), 153, 157, 159, 170, 171, 183, 206, 207; **Shuttermecki Photography LLC:** Anne Brink, 66; **Shutterstock:** 97, 111; **Skip Willits Fine Art Photography:** 102; **Katharine Spigarelli:** 182; **Sri Sri Radha Krishna Temple:** 262; **State of Tennessee Photographic Services:** 93; **Jocelyn Stewart:** 11 (top); **Keith Stokes:** 180; **SuperStock:** age fotostock, 6–7, 19 (bottom), 91 (top), 254, 260; David Forbert, 44; Hidekazu Nishibata, 112 (bottom); Kurt Scholz, 258; Underwood Photo Archives, 57 (right); **The Telfair Enterprise:** Kelley M. Arnold, 106; **Tinkertown Museum:** 212, 213; **Tom Till Photography:** 76–77, 101, 195 (center); **Transparencies, Inc.:** Jack Harris, 98; Ford Smith, 232; **Wesley Treat:** 220 (bottom), 227; **Elwin Trump:** 164, 231; **UCM Museum:** 129 (bottom); **Unicorn Stock Photos:** Deneve Feigh Bunde, 169; Dave G. Houser, 244; Andre Jenny, 194; Chuck Schmeiser, 230; Jim Shippee, 247; Aneal Vohra, 184; **Uniroyal® Tire:** 140; **Don Voelker:** 144, 145, 146; **Andrea Wells:** 299; **Witch History Museum:** Nancy Hurrell, 26 (left); **www.woodmaninstitutemuseum.org:** 34, 35; **Wyoming Travel & Tourism:** 252; **Zanesville COC:** 135

---

**Jeff Bahr** is a reporter for *The County Seat* and the coauthor of *Weird Virginia*. A contributing writer for several offbeat books including *Weird U.S.*, *Weird Pennsylvania*, *Weird New York*, and *Armchair Reader™: Weird, Scary & Unusual*, he hunts for writing fodder in America's strangest places.



Louis Weber, CEO
Publications International, Ltd.
7373 North Cicero Avenue
Lincolnwood, Illinois 60712



ISBN-13: 978-1-4127-1683-3
ISBN-10: 1-4127-1683-7

Manufactured in China.

8 7 6 5 4 3 2 1

Library of Congress Control Number: 2008936553

Frog Bridge, Willimantic, Connecticut

Burning Man Festival, Black Rock Desert, Nevada

Queen Califia's Magical Circle, Escondido, California

Lucy the Elephant, Margate, New Jersey

## *Introduction*

# HIT THE ROAD!

America is a land chock-full of oddities. There are perhaps as many reasons for this as there are people behind them, and therein lies a clue. The United States is a grand melting pot, blending cultures, religions, outlooks, and perspectives at a level far above that of most countries. It stands to reason, then, that such a vast assemblage of people, backgrounds, and personalities will lead to creations that are both amazing and unusual—not to mention weird!

But this represents just a portion of the picture. To simply dismiss the creators of the odd as "strange" is to do them a great disservice. It pays to remember that inventor Thomas Edison was once branded a mental incompetent, and painter Vincent van Gogh was deemed a raving lunatic. And yet, both "odd ducks" managed to change our world for the better despite their inherent "strangeness." Clearly a "one-size-fits-all" treatment of those who stand apart often misses the point.

That's where a book like *Amazing and Unusual USA* comes in. It's a celebration of the people and things that don't quite fit the mold—the attractions (and the artists behind them) that astound, amaze, and captivate. From the bizarre and eccentric to the amusing and downright scary, you'll find an astounding collection of everything offbeat.

Consider, for example, the World's Oldest Edible Cured Ham. What could be more delightful (or maybe "repulsive" is a better word?) than a pet ham? This one is 106 years old and is located in Smithfield, Virginia. Boy, is it ever gamy!

If you're looking for something a bit more colorful (and less likely to cause food poisoning!), head over to Queen Califia's Magical Circle *(pictured)*. This playful sculpture garden is bound to capture your imagination. And who knows—maybe it will even inspire you to create something amazing and unusual of your very own.

There's a whole wide, weird world out there just waiting to be explored. So come on—leave behind the expected and mundane and experience a sub-America little known to most but beloved by many. *Amazing and Unusual USA* is your passport to discovery.

# Chapter One
# NEW ENGLAND

America got its start in New England. As a result, this relatively small region packs quite a wallop. From the English pilgrims who established America's new colonies and government to the entrepreneurial spirit that faced down repeated hardships to emerge victorious, the six states that comprise New England are brimming with resolve.

This region also features its share of weirdness. Is bad art your thing? You can get your fill (swill?) at the Museum of Bad Art in Dedham, Massachusetts. Maybe bad weather sounds a bit more exciting? Take the Auto Road to the top of New Hampshire's Mount Washington. With a 231-mile-per-hour wind gust recorded topside in 1934, Mount Washington blows harder than any other place on planet Earth.

Taking cues from its populace, New England often peppers its oddities with bits of high society. To see such regal living up close, consider the Lizzie Borden Bed & Breakfast Museum in Fall River, Massachusetts. Just make sure to hold onto your head when you do. Thwack!

*Brookfield Floating Bridge, Brookfield, Vermont*

## Eartha, the World's Largest Rotating Globe

***Yarmouth, Maine***

What could put a mapmaking firm on the map? The world's largest globe, of course. DeLorme, a company best known for its road atlases, decided to puff its chest by taking its cartography prowess to the next level. At the company's national headquarters in Yarmouth, designers unearthed "Eartha." According to company spokespeople, the enormous globe features the "largest image of earth ever created."

Housed in a three-story glass atrium, the brightly colored marble is a sight to behold. Launched into orbit in 1998, the sphere appears to the earthbound eye much as it would to a space traveler. Vivid colors replicate topography, vegetation, major roadways, and cities. Shading suggests ocean depths. In a nod to accuracy, the sphere actually rotates and revolves.

At 41.5 feet in diameter, Eartha is recognized by *Guinness World Records* as the "World's Largest Revolving/Rotating Globe." Says DeLorme: "Eartha will instill a sense of wonder in people when they first see it and we hope they walk away from it with a better appreciation and knowledge of the world around them."

**AND THE WINNER IS....**

The honor of World's Largest (stationary) Globe belongs to the Unisphere in Queens, New York. It is 120 feet in diameter.

**Move Over, Italy!**

Before Eartha, Italy held the record for the World's Largest Revolving Globe. The Globe of Peace, located in Apeccio, Italy, is 33 feet in diameter.

## The Desert of Maine

***Freeport, Maine***

Despite accusations to the contrary, the owners of the "Desert of Maine" attraction insist, "No, we didn't dump it here!"

Geologists claim that there's really no mystery. A glacier supposedly slid through the area 11,000 years ago and left behind the sand and mineral deposits that today are known as the Desert of Maine.

An alternate explanation holds that bad farming practices were responsible for the desert. In this scenario, sand dunes infiltrated open fields not protected by a layer of grass, much like what occurred during America's "dust bowl" days.

So, who's right? We believe the proper answer is: Who really cares? When you locate a desert in a rainy northern state like Maine, you enjoy it for all it's worth.

Narrated coach tours offer visitors an opportunity to "dig" the sand for themselves. Those who prefer a more solitary adventure can take a walking tour on marked nature trails. A couple of bucks are all that separate the masses from this "famous natural phenomenon." What more do we need to know?

**QUICK FACT**

Visitors to the Desert of Maine will also find a museum featuring a collection of different sands from all over the world.

## Paul Bunyan Statue and Birthplace

***Bangor, Maine***

We wanted to cram the "world's biggest" everything into this book, so it's only fitting that we include the Paul Bunyan statue up in Bangor, Maine. This hardy fellow stands some 31 feet tall and strains scale springs with his 3,700-pound heft.

The giant lumberjack has been standing in Bangor since 1959. Armed with an equally enormous ax and pick, this figure is reputed to be the largest statue of Paul Bunyan in the world. How do we know this? It says so right on the base.

### The Legend of Paul Bunyan

Legend has it that giant lumberjack Paul Bunyan weighed a whopping 80 pounds when five storks delivered him as a baby. He grew up so fast that he was wearing his father's clothes within a week. Paul grew up on the coast of Maine but relocated with Babe, his famous blue ox sidekick, to Minnesota. There, the young and rambunctious duo created the state's 10,000 lakes with their horseplay. Later, Paul went on to invent the logging industry and chop down vast tracts of forest single-handedly.

### He's Everywhere!

Big Paul might just be the mascot of the American road. He's the subject of so many statues and woodcarvings that we simply didn't have room for them all. A few of the notable ones reside in Bemidji and Brainerd, Minnesota; Bangor, Maine; Klamath, California; and Ossineke, Michigan.

(Left) *Klamath, California's tribute to Paul and his big, blue friend.* (Below) *Paul and Babe also call Bemidji, Minnesota, home.*

## Old Lobster Fisherman

***Boothbay Harbor, Maine***

A fitting mascot for Brown's Wharf Restaurant, Motel & Marina, this stoic, yellow-clad angler consists of wood, steel, and fiberglass and measures 25 feet from boot to cap.

He's worn the same contemplative look since 1967, the year that Brown's Wharf landlocked him. Maybe the crusty one's plotting a return to the sea?

**QUICK FACT**

Brown's Wharf has been owned and operated by the Brown family for more than 50 years.

## Evergreen Cemetery's Grave with a Window

***New Haven, Vermont***

In 17th-century America, the fear of being buried alive was very real. In those days, medical testing procedures that could positively confirm death were scarce.

Perhaps knowing this, Timothy Clark Smith is spending eternity six feet underground in a "safety coffin," a device designed to give him a second chance if he happened to be buried before his time. Staring straight up through a tube that's capped with a glass plate, Smith was laid to rest in Evergreen Cemetery in 1893.

In addition to his picture window, Smith was buried with a bell in one hand to signal for help had his burial been premature. Since no ringing noises were ever reported at the cemetery, we'll assume that Smith's entombment was, in fact, merited. Thank goodness!

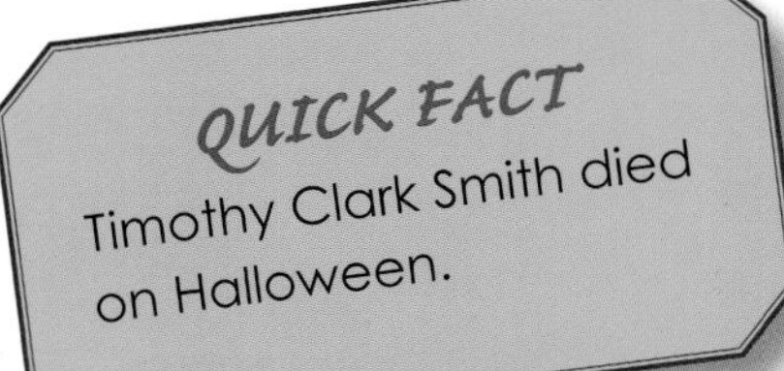

## Dog Chapel

***St. Johnsbury, Vermont***

Just after artist Stephen Huneck survived a near-death experience, he claims to have had a vision. According to Huneck, he was instructed to build a dog chapel: "a place where people can go and celebrate the spiritual bond they have with their dogs."

Accepting the vision at face value, Huneck constructed his dog chapel in 2000. Since then, St. Johnsbury canines and their owners have grown ever closer, sitting side by side in the chapel's pews or moving freely among its 400 scenic acres.

Doggy sculptures are spread throughout and include canine heads mounted on pillars, a winged dog affixed to the chapel's steeple—even a businessman taking Fido out for a walk.

Huneck also saw fit to include nature trails and swimming ponds in his doggy retreat—all the better to set the mood for enlightenment.

After such embraced spirituality, man (or woman) and best friend can check out Huneck's prints or snap up a copy of his *Dog Chapel* book. At this chapel, it truly is a dog's life.

**QUICK FACT**

Huneck died in 2010. The chapel is still open and run by his wife, Gwen.

## Knight's Spider Web Farm

***Williamstown, Vermont***

Peter Parker, a.k.a. Spider-Man, has nothing at all on *Spiderwebman*, a.k.a. Will Knight. While the former was only bitten by an arachnid, the latter lives among his eight-legged friends and makes his living off their webs. He even resides on Spider Web Farm Road.

Knight first thought of harvesting spiderwebs in the 1970s. Teaming up with artist wife Terry, the former cabinetmaker set out to capture the artistry of spiderwebs by mounting them on wood backgrounds.

To obtain his webs, Knight hangs custom-built racks in his backyard. In the morning, after the spiders have done what spiders do, Knight very gingerly paints the sticky webs, then transfers them to wooden plaques. Once this is accomplished, he seals the webs with lacquer, sends them off to be painted with artistic flowers and the like, and *voilà*, spider art is born.

**QUICK FACT**

While Knight takes his tacky business very seriously, he's not above a little fun. His Web site instructs visitors to "Browse a 'real web' for a change." Indeed.

*The museum's visitor center is located inside the Round Barn.*

*The Electra Havemeyer Webb Memorial Building houses the museum's impressive collection of Impressionist paintings.*

## Shelburne Museum

***Shelburne, Vermont***

The U.S. military possesses an explosive device known as the Mother of All Bombs (MOAB). It is called that simply because it's the largest nonnuclear bomb ever built. The Shelburne Museum, a celebrated Vermont institution where practically everything is featured, might be better served if it were called MOAM, short for mother of all museums. It is *that* big. It takes 45 full acres and 39 buildings to display the museum's collection, and that's with much of it overflowing onto the grounds.

Founded in 1947, the museum was created by Electra Havemeyer Webb (1888–1960), daughter of Henry O. Havemeyer (1847–1907), who founded the Domino Sugar Company. With near limitless resources, Webb acquired an eclectic smorgasbord of items over her lifetime; her collection was some 80,000 objects strong at the time of her death.

These and approximately 70,000 additional items are now housed at the Shelburne Museum in the Lake Champlain Valley. So, just how big is this place? One of the most revered items found within this hodgepodge is the 1906 steamship *Ticond-*

*eroga*. This is no mock-up or reproduction but rather an actual 220-foot-long side-wheel steamer. Webb had it transported from Lake Champlain to the museum, where it's been entertaining visitors since 1955.

Another crowd-pleaser is the Colchester Point Lighthouse. Built in 1871, the Lake Champlain structure originally marked three reefs between Vermont and New York. It was dismantled, reassembled at the museum, and today recalls 19th-century life on the lake.

In addition to these showstoppers, visitors will find Impressionist paintings featuring works by Monet and Degas, historic house interiors from 1790–1950, decorative art, folk art, decoys, carriages, tools, dolls and dollhouses, toys, quilts, Native American artifacts—the list goes on and on and on. All are contained within eye-pleasing grounds that represent an idyllic slice of Americana. We'd expect no less from the MOAM.

*Rare, 19th-century stencil designs are on display at the Stencil House.*

*Inside the Horseshoe Barn, visitors find a large collection of 19th- and 20th-century vehicles, including a Conestoga wagon.*

## Phineas Gage Memorial

***Cavendish, Vermont***

On September 13, 1848, an event occurred that was so very freakish it could turn Robert L. Ripley into a disbeliever. Phineas Gage, a railroad foreman, was setting charges when one of the explosives accidentally detonated. The resulting blast drove an iron rod more than three feet long into his head. The unlikely projectile pierced just below his eye, continued through the top of his skull, and skewered his brain in the process. Gage should have died. But by some miracle, he survived. In fact, he soon regained consciousness and was able to speak on his way to the hospital.

Today, a memorial celebrates Gage's astonishing recovery while also pointing to lessons learned from the incident. Despite living 12 years beyond that fateful day, the plaque tells how Gage's personality was affected, turning him from a hard-working and well-liked man into a shiftless sort who behaved inappropriately and swore incessantly. Finally, medical science had credible evidence that the brain directly affects behavior. The stage for brain mapping had been set.

The monument is located in an empty lot less than one mile from the accident site. (Directions to the actual spot are detailed on the memorial.) Through misfortune came a greater understanding of the human brain. Phineas Gage made it possible.

## Brookfield Floating Bridge

***Brookfield, Vermont***

Anyone who has crossed Vermont's Brookfield Floating Bridge by car is well aware of its treachery. Anyone who has attempted the same by motorcycle probably took an unplanned swim. This is what happens when a bridge crosses a lake that occasionally crosses *it*.

The 300-foot-long wooden Brookfield Bridge rests on 380 plastic barrels filled with Styrofoam that were designed to adjust to the level of Sunset Lake and keep the bridge deck high and dry. But more often than not, they allow the bridge to "sink" several inches below the surface of the water. To a visitor seeing the bridge for the first time, it appears as if an enormous engineering error has been made. Crossing the span does little to convince otherwise.

Why does this bridge float in the first place? Sunset Lake is far too deep to support a traditional, pillared span. Since 1820, impromptu "water ballet" maneuvers have been taking place as vehicles slowly amble across. And every once in a while, a motorcyclist goes kerplunk!

**QUICK FACT**

Bridge inspections conducted in 2008 caused officials to shut the bridge to vehicular traffic (though it was still open to pedestrians). Engineers were working to determine what repairs needed to be made.

## Hood Milk Bottle

***Boston, Massachusetts***

Built in 1930 to hawk homemade ice cream, this giant milk bottle was originally some 40 feet tall. In its middle years, it fell into neglect and was acquired by H. P. Hood and Sons, a noted dairy concern. The company refurbished it and donated it to the Boston Children's Museum in 1977.

These days, it has been refitted for snack-bar duty. One can only imagine how often "Got milk?" is "uddered" in its presence.

## The Mapparium

***Boston, Massachusetts***

Before Eartha (see page 8) came to be, the Mapparium was the preeminent exercise in global largesse.

The colorful globe is a representation of our world when seen from the inside out. Actually, it's the political world of 1935 as interpreted by its builder, Boston architect Chester Lindsay Churchill.

Viewed from a 30-foot glass bridge that traverses its middle, the three-story, stained-glass globe is comprised of 608 concave glass panels and is illuminated by hundreds of lights positioned around it. It's housed inside the Mary Baker Eddy Library, where tour guides explain its reason for being.

"By standing on the crystal bridge, one sees our planet from pole to pole with none of the distortion of area and distance that occur on a flat map," they explain rather matter-of-factly. What do we say? Never has a journey to the center of the earth come easier or cheaper. It may be a bit dated, but what's not to like?

**QUICK FACT**

Since its creation in 1935, the Mapparium has attracted more than ten million visitors.

## Jordan's Furniture Store and Trapeze School

***Reading, Massachusetts***

If you find that shopping for furniture leaves a little something to be desired, you might want to check out Jordan's Furniture Store. Its outlet in Reading happens to feature a trapeze school. Makes perfect sense to us.

Like any good furniture "circus," Jordan's also features a sideshow. "Beantown" offers a wall covered with jelly beans, while the "Green Monster" features a giant rendition of Boston's Fenway Park mascot squeezing the life out of a New York Yankee. Encircling such fun bits are the expected furniture shopping opportunities and—of course—the trapeze school itself.

If not put off by its array of 30-foot towers and safety nets, anyone can sign up to take a swing. There's even an area where well-wishers (or those who wish for the swinger's early demise) can cheer their heroes on.

Now, about that futon . . . .

## Museum of Bad Art

### *Dedham, Massachusetts*

If one longs to visit an art museum that self-appointed sophisticates will avoid like the plague, a trip to Boston's Museum of Bad Art (MOBA) is the ticket. The museum, which celebrates the very *worst* in self-expression, began with a terrible painting that founder Scott Wilson retrieved from the trash in 1993. Whimsically titled *Lucy in the Field with Flowers,* it depicts an elderly woman in a frumpy housedress performing an off-kilter dance in a field of flowers.

Somehow, Wilson was able to see beyond the painting's bile-inducing veneer and into its very soul. "The motion, the chair, the sway of her breast, the subtle hues of the sky, the expression on her face—every detail combines to create this transcendent and compelling portrait, every detail cries out 'masterpiece,' " declares Wilson. Ahem, we'll take his word for it.

With entire collections found under divisions of portraiture, landscapes, and "unseen forces" (a conglomeration of truly horrendous styles), a museum visitor is never far from a belly laugh or stomach upset. "Art too bad to be ignored" is the museum's slogan, and believe us, these fine folks are *not* exaggerating.

Lucy in the Field with Flowers *by Unknown*

Green Cowboy *by Martha*

Guarding the Rock *by Unknown*

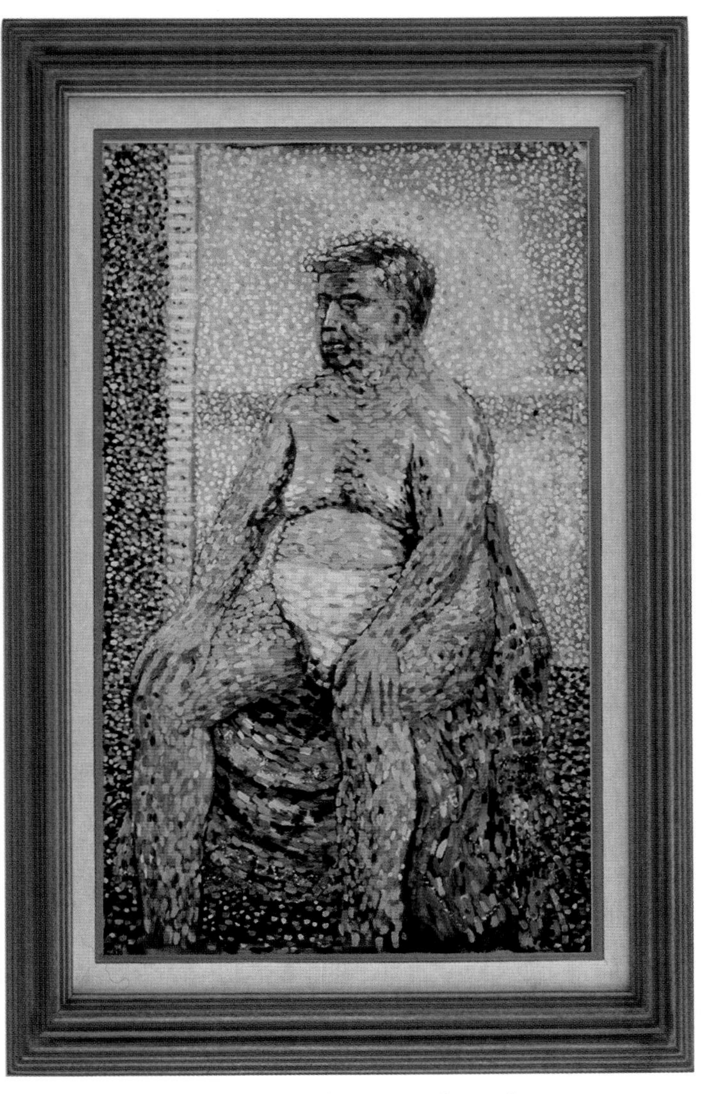

Sunday on the Pot with George *by Unknown*

## Dr. Seuss National Memorial Sculpture Garden

***Springfield, Massachusetts***

Who could ever forget such books as *Green Eggs and Ham* or *The Cat in the Hat?* Dr. Seuss, a.k.a. Theodor Seuss Geisel (1904–1991), produced zany books that children actually wanted to read. As a result, the offbeat writer from Springfield, Massachusetts, has become a beloved legend. Recognizing this, his hometown raised more than $6 million to create a national memorial in his honor.

Geisel's stepdaughter, Lark Grey Dimond-Cates, sculpted bronze figures of Seuss's most beloved characters. These include the Lorax, Thidwick the Big-Hearted Moose, the Grinch and his dog Max, Horton the Elephant, and of course, the Cat in the Hat. There's even a sculpture of Geisel at his drawing board engrossed in the process of liberating his youthful followers.

**QUICK FACT**

Dr. Seuss wasn't actually a doctor at all. Although Oxford-educated, the budding writer failed to snare a sheepskin. The "Dr." in his pen name is a nod to his father's unfulfilled hopes in this area.

*Dr. Seuss and his famed Cat in the Hat*

*This sculpture, dubbed* The Storyteller, *is backed by text from* Oh, the Places You'll Go!

### But Did They Rhyme?

Dr. Seuss's books have been translated into more than 15 different languages. Seems like some mighty challenging translating work to us!

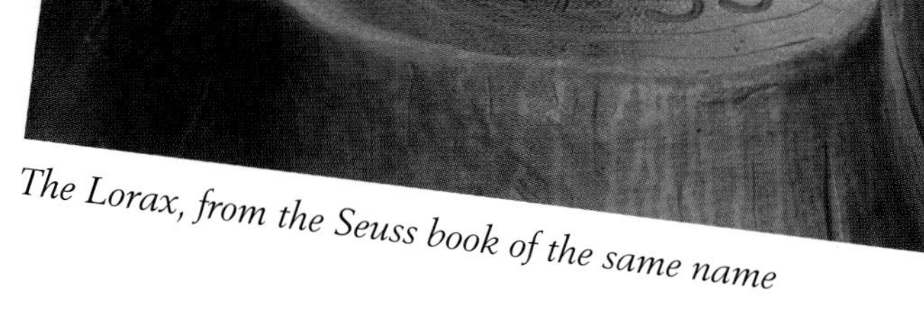

*The Lorax, from the Seuss book of the same name*

## Witch History Museum

***Salem, Massachusetts***

If a visitor wishes to get up close and personal with the witch hysteria of the late 1600s, this is the place. With first-person narrations and an unsettling basement diorama featuring devil-possessed girls dancing with wild abandon, the Witch History Museum centers on little-known stories from the witching era.

The "Graveyard" and "Witch in the Night" dioramas are particularly creepy. As are the voice tracks that seem to come from nowhere. While a visit to this bewitching spot is advised, perhaps it's best done in pairs. Yikes!

**QUICK FACT**

Nineteen "witches" were put to death in 1692.

**QUICK FACT**
The House of the Seven Gables features a mysterious hidden staircase.

## House of the Seven Gables

### *Salem, Massachusetts*

In the 1851 novel *The House of the Seven Gables,* American author Nathaniel Hawthorne (1804–1864) alludes to a "rusty wooden house, with seven acutely peaked gables." In real life, the house was known as the Turner-Ingersoll Mansion, though today it goes by the name of the novel that made it famous.

This 1668 dwelling in Salem's witch country has become famous for its longevity (it's thought to be the oldest surviving 17th-century wooden mansion in New England), as well as for its interesting features. It's listed on the National Register of Historic Places, and tours of its many rooms are available.

These days, Nathaniel Hawthorne's birth house has been relocated to the grounds, and a museum featuring more than 2,000 artifacts completes the lure.

## Lizzie Borden Bed & Breakfast Museum

***Fall River, Massachusetts***

Lizzie Borden took an ax,
And gave her mother forty whacks.
And when she saw what she had done,
She gave her father forty-one.

*The Borden House in Fall River, Massachusetts*

August 4, 1892, began quite uncomfortably for the Borden family. Rather mysteriously, family members had been stricken with food poisoning and were in more than a little distress. However, Andrew Borden, one of Fall River's wealthiest men, and his second wife, Abby, would soon encounter an even worse fate—an ax-wielding murderer was in their midst.

Daughter Lizzie was the first person to discover her father's lifeless body. She screamed to a maid, "Come down quick—father's dead. Somebody came in and killed him!" Soon, Lizzie and a neighbor would discover the mangled body of Abby Borden who, like her husband Andrew, had been bludgeoned to death. After an investigation, Lizzie Borden was charged with the crimes.

Borden was eventually acquitted on all charges, even though history shows there was a preponderance of evidence. Such knowledge is standard fare more than a century later. What is not standard is the fact that the Borden house still exists. It currently operates as a bed-and-breakfast, of all bizarre things, and actually encourages people to *sleep* in and move about the infamous "death" rooms.

The home features six bedrooms (one of them the room where Abby Borden went all to pieces), and visitors are invited to "learn the true facts about Lizzie Borden and the murders of 1892."

The parlor where Andrew Borden met the business end of an ax is also open to guests. What first appears to be the actual couch upon which he was bludgeoned is revealed to be a reproduction. Visitors soon learn that there was "way too much blood" on the original piece.

The tour is given by guides extremely well-versed in the murders. When one of them is asked if she believes Lizzie to be guilty or innocent, her words leave her lips with a measured cadence, with much thought and knowledge clearly applied to the answer. "In my opinion, Lizzie Borden was undoubtedly. . . ."

Be sure to swing by for the answer. Chop, chop.

*Lizzie's bedroom*

*A replica of the couch on which Andrew Borden was killed*

# Mount Washington

***New Hampshire***

If you were asked to name the place on planet Earth responsible for the world's worst weather, we'd guess the state of New Hampshire would *not* be on your short list. This would be an oversight on your part. Though comparatively small, Mount Washington (a.k.a. the "killer mountain") is capable of more harshness than any granite lump has a right to be.

First, a look at the facts: 6,288-foot Mount Washington is located at a spot where three major storm tracks regularly collide. Due to this collision and a funneling effect attributed to its unique topography (its tree line occurs at a comparatively low 5,000 feet), the mountain produces scary, strong winds. How scary? The mountain's weather is so freakish that a

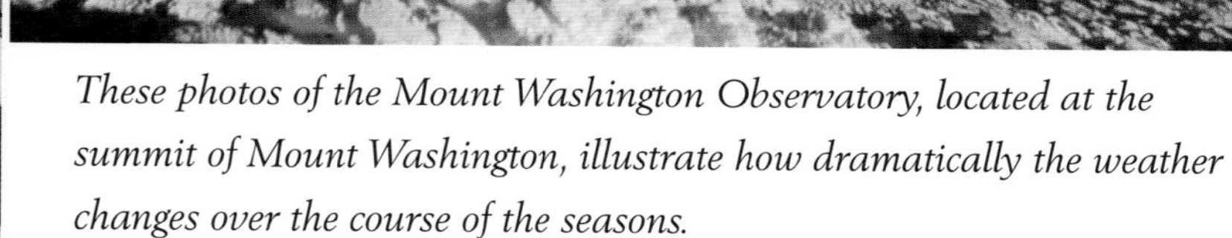

*These photos of the Mount Washington Observatory, located at the summit of Mount Washington, illustrate how dramatically the weather changes over the course of the seasons.*

year-round weather observatory has existed at its summit since 1870. In the early days, buildings were actually chained to the mountain to save them from being blown off of it. This sort of thing can happen in an environment where hurricane-force winds occur just about every third day throughout the year.

On April 12, 1934, as if to prove its windy superiority, the mountain let loose with a gust of 231 miles per hour. This was—and still is—the greatest nontornado blast ever measured on Earth. But wind represents only a portion of Mount Washington's mayhem. Fast-changing weather adds to its knockout blow.

In 1855, 23-year-old Lizzie Bourne and two relatives began a hike to the mountain's summit. The plan was to spend the night at the Tip Top House. They would walk along the precursor to Mount Washington's famed Auto Road, a steep path that climbs out of the valley and tags the top of the mountain.

Nearing exhaustion after many hours of exertion, the party finally broke tree line and came within sight of the summit cone. They decided to push on. Almost immediately, windswept rain and plummeting temperatures dogged their attempts. With thick fog shrouding their goal, the party stopped and dug in for a hellish night. Survival was now their chief interest.

It would be Lizzie's last climb. She had underestimated the power of the mountain and died of exposure. But she could hardly be blamed for such foolhardiness. The September day of her death had started off like many other summer days that preceded it, quite warm and sunny. The most heartbreaking part? She and her group had made it to within a few hundred yards of the Tip Top House. Unfortunately, the mountain's cruel weather had completely masked the object of their salvation.

The Sherman Adams Visitor's Center located at Mount Washington's summit features more than 100 names of other deaths on the mountain. It proves that killers can and do come in all sizes. How about a hike?

Despite a grisly "death statistic" board at the mountain's summit, Mount Washington remains a hiking mecca. Each year, thousands of "peak-baggers" climb up and down the imposing mountain and end up none the worse for wear. The Appalachian Mountain Club (AMC) maintains the Pinkham Notch Visitor's Center at Mount Washington's base. Rangers will tell you that climbs here are as safe as climbers make them, and that proper gear and an eye on weather are essential. Nevertheless, incidents do occur. This fear factor no doubt adds to Mount Washington's allure.

**QUICK FACT**

The Tip Top House is a summit hotel that was built in 1853. Although it no longer accommodates overnight guests, the Tip Top House is still open to visitors as a historic site.

## Mud Bowl Championships

***North Conway, New Hampshire***

Up in New England, touch football has deep roots. The Kennedy boys (yes, *those* Kennedys) helped popularize the game at their Hyannisport compound. However, the Mud Bowl Championships ran the Kennedys' regal approach right into the dirt. Make that wet dirt, as in mud.

Each September since 1975, teams have gathered in North Conway to get down and dirty. Before the official game begins, a pep rally, bonfire, and "drunkfest" instill the proper mood. As is plain to see, "Here's mud in your eye" has multiple meanings up in these parts.

The "Hogs," a mud bowl team out of North Conway, have proven their superiority over the years. So much so that they've since constructed the "Hog Coliseum" to host the event. If rain dampens their playing field, that's swell. If not, sprinklers get the job done. Let the filthy games begin!

**QUICK FACT**
The Hog Coliseum is the only mud football stadium in the world.

## Ruggles Mine

***Grafton, New Hampshire***

The "World Famous" Ruggles Mine combines good old-fashioned American hucksterism with a captivating environment worthy of a visit. The "Mine in the Sky," as the brochure reads, is billed as "the oldest and most spectacular mica, feldspar, beryl, and uranium mine in the USA."

Opened to the public in 1963, the place is so cavernous that human beings look like fire ants beside its honeycombed tunnels. This lends the mine's "most spectacular" boast much credence and can easily leave one spellbound.

Visitors interested in searching for such prized minerals as gummite and autunite can rent hammers on site.

## Woodman Institute Museum

***Dover, New Hampshire***

*An exterior view of the Woodman Institute*

*The museum's quirkiness is not limited to the indoor exhibits!*

The Woodman Institute has been called a museum's museum. The reason for this goes beyond its prized four-legged chicken and past its 1776 tax bill from King George to the citizens of Dover. It's the variety that separates the place.

With the 1818 Woodman House and other brick structures acting as hosts, artifacts of every type and every stripe line the facility. Here's a pocket watch once carried by Josiah Bartlett, signer of the Declaration of Independence; there's a horse saddle that once touched the tushie of President Abraham Lincoln. The fun lies in never knowing what comes next.

Upon her death in 1915, Annie E. Woodman got the ball rolling when she bequeathed $100,000, along with her home, to create a worthy Dover institution. The museum got its start in 1916. Since then, it has acquired such eclectic offerings as Native American artifacts, preserved mammals, glassware, china, pewter, police and firefighting equipment, as well as the infamous stuffed four-legged chicken. The latter is actually a cute-as-a-button chick—but no matter. If thrills are sought, a two-headed snake can be found just a few rows over. Such is the Woodman Institute.

The last cougar to be killed in New Hampshire

A 50,000-year-old mastodon tooth

A sampling from the museum's mineral collection

The Institute's famous four-legged chicken

## Clark's Trading Post

***Lincoln, New Hampshire***

Long before there were theme parks to amuse travelers, one-off places like Clark's Trading Post ruled the roost. Each operation was as individual and unique as its operators, and you could never be certain what you'd happen upon next.

"Ed Clark's Eskimo Sled Dog Ranch," the original operation begun by Florence and Ed Clark in 1928, featured purebred Eskimo sled dogs. The couple's intent was to bring the far north into New Hampshire's White Mountains—a rough and ready region that attracted outdoor types. In 1931, Ed purchased a live black bear and put it on display. More than any attraction before it, the bear lured so many visitors that more bears were quickly added.

Eventually, sons Murray and Edward began working with the bruins. In 1949, they formed a show that featured bear antics and infused it with wit and educational bits for balance. Clark's bear show was born.

Visitors would come from all parts to witness the critters drinking from beer cans, swinging on swings, and shooting "bear-sketballs." With an infusion of capital, the operation eventually changed its name to Clark's Trading Post and grew to include a steam-powered train ride, a Russian circus troupe, even a much-beloved, if at first off-putting, human "Wolfman."

Through the years, as perceptions of animal cruelty evolved, Clark's Trading Post came under scrutiny. According to the family, such concerns are completely baseless. They point to the fact that no bear is ever forced to perform. As to concerns about the trainers' well-being, the family patriarch W. Murray Clark explains that every family member has been injured—a fact that causes them to take their jobs very seriously. Nevertheless, they treat the bears with great affection and believe that such goes a long way toward keeping the animals content and less likely to attack.

*Visitors to Clark's Trading Post enjoy the legendary bear show* (above)*—not to mention the performance of the Russian circus troupe* (left).

This grand throwback to roadside attractions just passed its 80th birthday, and from all indications, it could go another 80 years. People never seem to tire of unique spots such as this. In fact, when it comes to popularity, Clark's Trading Post has "bearly" scratched the surface.

## World's Largest Bug

***Providence, Rhode Island***

How do you make the world's largest bug even more lovable? Design him as a termite and give him the name "Nibbles Woodaway." At 58 feet long, we don't suppose many people would contest Nibbles's grandiose claim of world superiority, particularly if they live in wood-framed houses.

But Nibbles is even tougher than his nibbling suggests. When built in 1980 at a cost of $30,000, the enormous winged creature was designed to withstand the force of a hurricane.

The giant bug's deep-blue hue easily catches the eye, and he's outfitted in different garb for major holidays. Somehow the thought of a 58-foot termite wearing an Uncle Sam hat appeals to us. You?

QUICK FACT

Not only is Providence the capital of Rhode Island—it's also the largest city in the state. What better place for the world's largest bug?

## Waterfire

***Providence, Rhode Island***

Waterfire, an environmental art installation, is made up of more than 100 bonfires that rage just above the three rivers (Woonasquatucket, Moshassuck, and Providence) of Waterplace Park. It's staged after dusk for maximum effect.

Created by artist Barnaby Evans in 1994, Waterfire blazes before an ever-changing background of classical and world music and offers visitors a uniquely artsy experience. The show sometimes draws as many as 65,000 people per night, a statistic that brings great joy to its creator.

It was Evans's deep fascination with liquid and flame that led to Waterfire. Says the artist: "Water will quench a fire, but fire can boil water away to invisibility." When combined, they can also entertain. A visit to Waterfire serves as scorching proof.

## Barker Character, Comic & Cartoon Museum

***Cheshire, Connecticut***

This nostalgic museum located in Cheshire tips its cap to beloved childhood icons such as Mickey and Minnie, the Flintstones, Charlie McCarthy, Li'l Abner, and, more recently, SpongeBob. The Connecticut museum houses the toys that founders Herb and Gloria Barker have accumulated over the years. They now have more than 80,000 items in their collection.

You'll see hundreds of Pez dispensers, 1,000 themed lunch boxes, 600 Disney and Ty Beanie Babies, several pieces of Pokémon memorabilia, and Lone Ranger and Roy Rogers toys of all types. It's a place meant for reminiscing—Dennis the Menace's "Mischief Kit"? It's here. Popeye collectibles? Sure! More than 3,000 Barbies? Present and accounted for. Rare tin toys? A whole case! Each exhibit displays the current market value of a collectible, but the toys are not for sale.

A theater shows short animated films from the 1930s and '40s featuring some of the beloved characters found in the museum. Large cartoon character cutouts are popular backdrops for photographs. An animation and sculpture gallery is located next door.

*The Barker Character, Comic & Cartoon Museum features a number of collectibles to stir up a sense of nostalgia. Its exhibits include many current favorites, as well as plenty that grown-ups will remember from their own childhoods.*

## Gillette Castle State Park

***East Haddam, Connecticut***

If the name sounds familiar, you're probably off track. This particular Gillette had nothing to do with shaving and everything to do with the stage.

Theater buffs may recall William Hooker Gillette (1853–1937), an American actor who delivered a memorable performance as Sherlock Holmes. If equally versed in castles, they'll also know that Gillette built himself a humdinger of a fortress high up on a bluff overlooking the Connecticut River.

Upon Gillette's death, his will stipulated that his circa-1919 castle not fall into the hands of any "blithering sap-head who has no conception of where he is or with what surrounded." In 1943, the actor got his wish when the state of Connecticut took possession of the unique property and christened it Gillette Castle State Park.

Since then, millions of visitors have gawked at the castle's stone exterior and admired its interior woodwork of southern white oak. With 14 dissimilar doors leading inside, visitors get a glimpse of a man who treasured uniqueness and creativity above all else.

**QUICK FACT**

The castle includes a system of hidden mirrors, which makes it possible to monitor the public areas from the master bedroom.

*These photographs of the castle's interior illustrate the grand beauty of Gillette's vision.*

## Dinosaur State Park

***Rocky Hill, Connecticut***

In 1966, some 2,000 dinosaur tracks were unearthed during excavation for a new state building. Realizing the importance of the find, the Connecticut Department of Environmental Protection took action. The result is Dinosaur State Park, a dino-centric spot where 500 of these impressions exist under a geodesic dome.

While no one can say with certainty just what species left the tracks (called *Eubrontes* by geologist Edward Hitchcock), scientists currently lean toward the carnivore Dilophosaurus. But the point is nearly moot. After some 200 million years, *whatever* left them is worthy of preservation—a fact underscored by the park's Registered National Landmark status.

**QUICK FACT**

Talk about a souvenir! Dinosaur State Park allows visitors to make plaster of paris casts of the dinosaur tracks. Be sure to check the park's Web site for a list of supplies you'll need to bring.

## New England Carousel Museum

***Bristol, Connecticut***

What goes around comes around, and what comes around at the New England Carousel Museum (NECM) keeps going and going and going. It appears the display's guardians would have it no other way.

If its title isn't descriptive enough, allow us to fill in the blanks. The NECM is a place that harkens back to a time before BlackBerries, iPhones, and theme parks. It speaks to the childish wonder in all of us through the magic of old-time carousels.

The museum's mission statement reads in part: "The New England Carousel Museum is dedicated to the acquisition, restoration and preservation of operating carousels and carousel memorabilia . . . ." Nicely put and fairly inclusive, but we think it can be simplified beyond this. Here goes: Did you ever get your chance to grab for the brass ring; to give your all in a free-spirited attempt at circle-clenching glory? As one of America's largest collections of antique carousels, this is one place that fully understands that primal desire. Perhaps you should give it a spin?

QUICK FACT
The bridge features four 11-foot frogs. Each frog cost a whopping $50,000!

## Frog Bridge

***Willimantic, Connecticut***

This whimsical bridge pays tribute to two disparate phenomena. The spools are monuments to the thread industry that was the backbone of the local economy in the 19th century. The frogs perched atop the spools are reminders of the infamous "Battle of the Frogs" of 1754, when the cries from dying, drought-ravaged bullfrogs seriously alarmed locals during the thick of the French and Indian War.

## The Children's Garbage Museum

***Stratford, Connecticut***

"This place is trashy!" says a visitor to the Children's Garbage Museum in Stratford. The remark is surprisingly positive. It describes a funky (in more ways than one) museum that seeks to tell the entire garbage story from trash can to landfill.

The museum accomplishes this with such exhibits as the giant compost pile (said to take one's breath away) and a recycling center that features recyclables viewed from an ultra-classy "sky box."

But the real showstopper is Trash-O-Saurus, a dinosaur made from a one-ton mound of trash. How or why a prehistoric beast factors into the trash picture is anyone's guess, but we assume even T-Rex wouldn't mess with "big stinky." Who would?

*Trash-O-Saurus*

### That's a Bunch of Garbage!

The Trash-O-Saurus wasn't made from a ton of garbage by happenstance. Rather, the number represents the amount of trash the average person throws out in a year.

LUCY
PARKING
ONLY
(ONE HR LIMIT)
ALL OTHERS TOWED
9 A.M. TO 9 P.M.
$55.00

# Chapter Two
# MID-ATLANTIC STATES

Made up of four states that rank among the most densely populated in the nation, the Mid-Atlantic region is an action-packed microcosm of America. Its topographic features include time-rounded green mountains, pastoral valleys, and a sparkling seacoast—a unique mixture not often found elsewhere.

This splendid diversity is mirrored in the region's people—a melting pot of humanity that's never at a loss for creativity or eccentricity. Testaments to this are found virtually everywhere and run the gamut from merely mild to absolutely wild.

By way of example, New York's Cardiff Giant in Cooperstown shows what can be accomplished with humor, ingenuity, and deception. God's Ark of Safety in Frostburg, Maryland, demonstrates faith at an extraordinarily elevated level, and the Pennsylvania coal town of Centralia (burning since 1962) proves that not *all* like it hot. In the Mid-Atlantic region, the more you probe, the more you're likely to find. The surprises just keep coming!

*Lucy the Elephant, Margate, New Jersey*

## Shoe House

***Hellam, Pennsylvania***

**QUICK FACT**

Haines must have had a soft spot for Fido. He included a shoe-shape doghouse on the site as well.

"There was an old woman who lived in a shoe—she had so many children she didn't know what to do."

This unique house—just off the famous Lincoln Highway—belongs in the land of enchantment. Haines Shoe House is a dead ringer for the boot in the popular nursery rhyme. And, yes, people have actually lived in it. But there is one notable difference. The circa-1949 house, 25 feet tall by 48 feet long, was *not* built to entertain children. It was built to hawk shoes.

Mahlon "The Shoe Wizard" Haines (1875–1962) operated 40 shoe stores in Pennsylvania and neighboring Maryland. While dreaming up sales gimmicks, Haines had a eureka moment. He decided to build a shoe-shape house and plaster his company's name on its side. Later, as a form of "giving back," Haines would make the shoe house available free of charge to elderly couples on weekends. The generous move boosted sales and earned Haines a sweet spot in people's hearts.

When Haines hung up his shoehorn, the building was sold. At various times thereafter, it became a private home, a museum, even an ice-cream parlor. Stained-glass windows in the shoe house depict Haines and his "soleful" purpose.

## Ringing Rocks

### *Upper Black Eddy, Pennsylvania*

As you pass through the hamlet of Upper Black Eddy, Pennsylvania, strange ringing noises will likely fill your ears. With not a bell in sight, you might believe you are developing tinnitus. Fear not. The ringing sounds are coming from an outside source—an ethereal place deeply shrouded in mystery.

The appropriately named Ringing Rocks Park is a 128-acre field of boulders. When struck with a rock or mallet, the rocks produce distinctly different tones—much like musical notes. Scientists will tell you that the 12,000-year-old rocks are composed of diabase, an igneous rock similar to volcanic basalt. Ringing Rocks is one of the largest concentrations of such rocks in the eastern United States. But this falls short of explaining *why* these rocks ring.

Unimpressed by something as trivial as scientific theory, music aficionados with hammers in hand swarm the park on weekends. Soon, the boulder field alights in a striking symphony of percussive sound. Could this be the origin of the term "rock concert"?

## Columcille

***Bangor, Pennsylvania***

With Celtic appreciation running high these days, it's little wonder that Columcille, an offbeat, mystical land of wonder, attracts so many people. Patterned after Scotland's Isle of Iona retreat, the 17-acre site features more than 80 oblong boulders (some as tall as 20 feet and weighing up to 45 tons) that protrude like proverbial sore thumbs. What do these megaliths represent? Different things to different people, according to Columcille's originators.

If this sounds confusing, it helps to understand that Columcille was designed with such ambiguity in mind. Founders William Cohea, Jr., and Frederick Lindkvist started Columcille in 1978 as "an open space to welcome people of all faiths and traditions interested in renewal and transformation."

The giant stones were "planted" to approximate the more than 350 found at the Isle of Iona. Cairns, stone altars, and chapels were added to the mix over the years. If the true meaning of the megaliths must be pinned down, this explanation lifted straight from Columcille's Web site may clear things up: "They [the stones] provide a sacred playground for the Human Spirit to dance, to encounter the mystery of the Earth's creation."

*St. Oran's Bell Tower*

An unnamed megalith

The Circle of Stones, with St. Oran's Bell Tower visible in the background

## The Old Jail Museum

***Jim Thorpe, Pennsylvania***

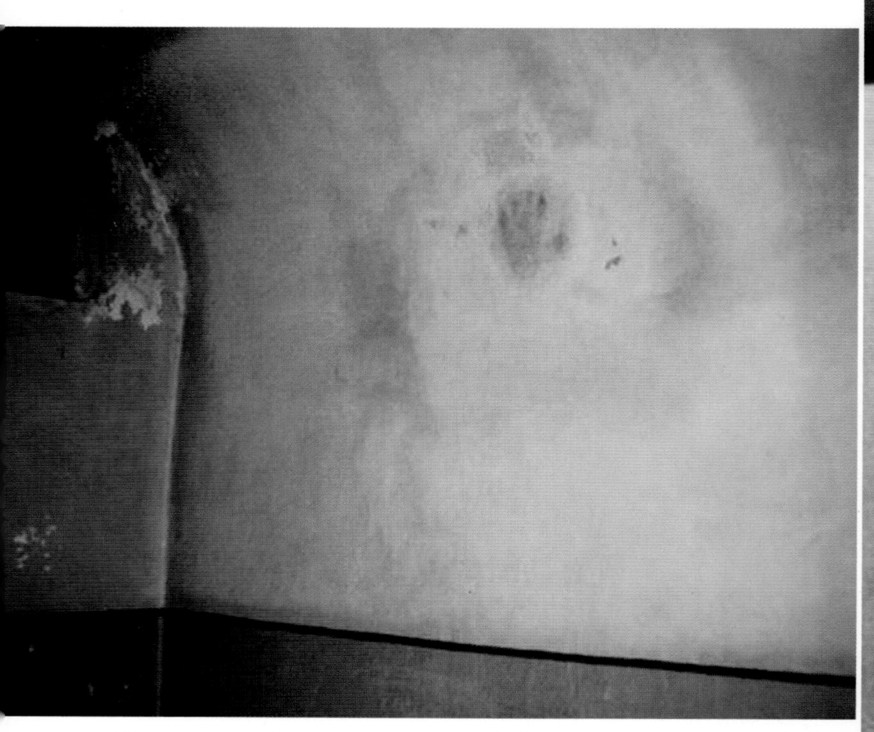

*The infamous handprint purportedly left by Alexander Campbell* (above) *is as chilling as cell 17 itself* (right).

The Old Jail Museum is a genuine throwback. Prisoners lived a decidedly stark existence inside its dungeonlike walls. Built in 1870, a time that stressed retribution over rehabilitation, the jail meted out justice in barbaric form. The prison also engaged in hangings. Some of these were more notorious than others, but none gained more fame than the execution of cell 17's prisoner Alexander Campbell in 1877.

Convicted as an accessory to murder, Campbell fervently declared his innocence. When he realized his plea had fallen on deaf ears, Campbell proclaimed: "I am innocent, and let this be my testimony." With that, the condemned man slammed his grimy hand against his cell wall and was led off to the gallows. Bizarrely, despite repeated painting and replastering, Campbell's handprint remains to this day.

The jail has long been closed but tours are provided to the public. It seems everyone wants to see cell 17 and the gallows where "innocent" Alexander Campbell drew his last breath. This, perhaps, represents Campbell's final solace.

## Centralia

***Pennsylvania***

When eastern Pennsylvanians refer to "the fire down below," they're probably not talking about the movie, the song, or even the saying. They're referring to Centralia, a town that was completely displaced by an underground mine fire.

The fire started in a landfill in 1962 and has been burning ever since. There's more than a little irony here, since the anthracite coal lying beneath Centralia is quite tricky to light. Once it catches, however, it's nearly impossible to extinguish. In Centralia's case, years of firefighting efforts couldn't stomp it out.

Due to the absurdly high risk of carbon monoxide poisoning, Centralia's 1,500 residents were eventually relocated to the nearby towns of Mt. Carmel and Ashland. As of 2007, only a handful of residents remained.

These days, there is nearly nothing left. Curious visitors will stop to watch smoke wafting up through ground fissures or to snoop around the few abandoned homes and businesses still standing in this hell on Earth. Then they'll leave. The scene is a far cry from the vibrant community that once existed here, but that idyllic memory speaks to another time and another town. Centralia has reverted to ashes.

No trip to Centralia would be complete without a visit to the Centralia portion of PA 54/61. On this strip, you'll find smoke rising from ground fissures that are so severe, the Pennsylvania Department of Transportation was forced to detour around this section in 1994. A few of these holes are so large they can swallow a human. Beware!

*These prison cells date back to 1929 and are similar to those still used at Sing-Sing today.*

## Sing-Sing Prison Museum

***Ossining, New York***

The saying "up the river" probably doesn't ring a bell with many these days, but that's probably a good thing. The reason? The aforementioned river is the mighty Hudson. And the place? None other than the dreaded Sing-Sing Prison. Surely no one wishes to remember such a ghastly place. Or do they?

Since the maximum-security prison remains an active facility, nosing around its walls might actually earn you a trip up the river. With this in mind, the town of Ossining opened the Sing-Sing Prison Museum. Inside, "prisonphiles" can learn all about life in the "Big House" (a term originally coined for Sing-Sing), including the history of the electric chair and the story behind the Rosenberg spy executions. Cell

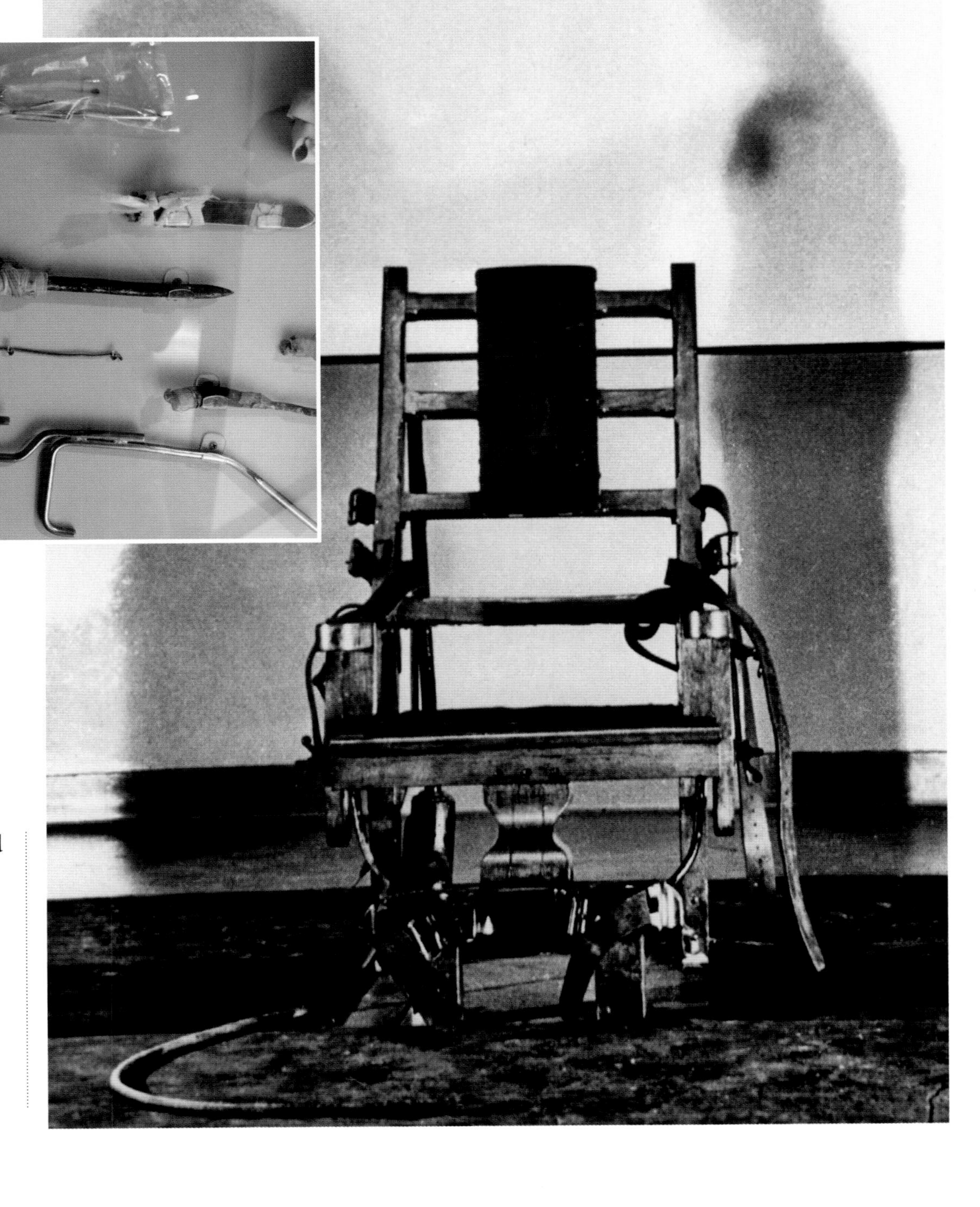


*The sinister prisoner weapon display* (above) *is every bit as chilling as "Old Sparky"* (right).

mock-ups and a replica of "Old Sparky" add to the macabre fun.

Sing-Sing remains an intimidating place, as illustrated by a prisoner weapons display at the museum, which features razor-sharp "shanks" that were confiscated from the prison. It seems there's never a "dull" moment at Sing-Sing *or* its museum.

## Boldt Castle

***Heart Island (Alexandria Bay), New York***

It's rather poetic that Boldt castle should be located on Heart Island, for it was built by a heart filled with love. George C. Boldt (1851–1916), manager of the New York's Waldorf-Astoria Hotel, loved his wife Louise so much that he decided to memorialize his devotion by presenting her with a dream castle.

For four splendid years, the Boldts and their children summered on Heart Island as the castle's construction advanced. The family marveled at the 6-story, 120-room bulk of the structure. Its mass was offset by ornate trim and flourishing Italian gardens. Unfortunately, in 1904, just as the castle was nearing completion, Louise died suddenly.

With his beloved wife taken from him, a heartbroken Boldt saw no reason to continue building an empty shrine. He ordered the castle's construction halted, and he never again set foot on the island.

The castle stood vacant for decades. Then, in 1977, the Thousand Islands Bridge Authority acquired the property and devised a funding mechanism to ensure that it would be preserved for future generations. Today, the castle's sad story is powerful enough to bring tears to the eyes of some visiting tourists. Perhaps this is the greatest testament to the power of one man's love.

## World's Largest Uncle Sam Statue

***Lake George, New York***

Uncle Sam, the red, white, and blue symbol of America, means different things to different people. Some view the "tall man with the tall hat" as an American mainstay—as integral to our nation as baseball. Others see Sam as a beggar whose hand is perpetually reaching into their wallets. "Here's Uncle Sam's cut," they'll grumble as they pay their taxes.

We're guessing the former applies at the Magic Forest Amusement Park in Lake George, New York. There, you'll find a 38-foot-tall Uncle Sam statue guarding the front gates.

Sam's resume shows that he has stood sentry over the Magic Forest since 1982. Before being relocated to Magic Forest, he watched over the 1981 Connecticut State Fair in Danbury. Beyond that, Sam's movements get murky. In the end, does it really matter? This Sam is large and in charge. America can sleep well tonight.

**QUICK FACT**

The phrase "Uncle Sam" dates back to the War of 1812. Legend has it that the origins of the name came from the troops' meat supplier, Samuel Wilson. However, other sources contend that the phrase is a play on the initials of the United States, especially since the first illustration of Uncle Sam didn't appear until 1852.

## Secret Caverns

### *Cobleskill, New York*

Have you heard the story of David and Goliath? If so, you'll instantly recall its message: "Small guy whips big guy." Secret Caverns, a kitschy show cave just outside of Albany, attempts this same feat each and every day. It has to. It's located farther along a road that first leads to its chief nemesis, Howe Caverns.

Despite being discovered later than "that other hole in the ground" and lacking its vast financial resources, Secret Caverns still entertains. Even the drive in is more fun than the drive to mainstream Howe, since Secret Caverns treats visitors to oodles of over-the-top signs. "Like a Limestone Cowboy" and "4 out of 5 Dentists Prefer Our Cavity" are just two examples.

When Secret Caverns tour guides are reminded of Howe's much-lauded underground boat ride, they usually reply, "big deal, *we* have a 100-foot underground waterfall!" It's completely true and a genuine oddity in its own right. So, "the little cavern that could" continues its fierce daily battle. Say, how did that David and Goliath story end again?

*The entrance to Secret Caverns offers a sneak preview to the weird wonders inside.*

*The natural beauty of Secret Caverns and its underground waterfall are a sight to behold.*

## Homer and Langley's Mystery Spot

***Phoenicia, New York***

In the interest of full disclosure we'll come right to the point. Despite its misleading name, Homer and Langley's Mystery Spot is an antique shop. But that's where any semblance of normality ends. The name alone gives a clue of what's to come. Homer and Langley were the infamous Collyer brothers, marvelously eccentric gents who lived among more than 100 tons of clutter. Today, proprietor Laura Levine carries on their tradition. She packs more bizarre stuff into her Phoenicia, New York, store than befits sanity.

But then sanity isn't the driving force here. Fun and profit are. Check out a painting of *Desdemona, the Devil Girl of Phoenicia*, who sports a cleft tongue and horns growing from her head. The piece oozes weirdness. How about a "creepy doll exhibit" that features a bisque baby doll in an egg? A bit unsettling, that one.

From the "Kingdom of Rusticalia" to the "Sub-Kingdom of Plasticalia," thousands of items abound, and most are for sale. We wouldn't be surprised if the Collyer brothers themselves were buried somewhere inside. For Laura Levine, hoarding's uncrowned queen, there could be no greater compliment.

**QUICK FACT**

Care to take a guess as to what the Mystery Spot's motto might be? If you guessed something close to "Clutter My World," you hit it right on the spot!

**Strange but True**

When the police were tipped to Homer's death, they were puzzled over the mysterious absence of Langley. A few days later, he was found; he'd been buried under the clutter he and his infamous brother had amassed.

QUICK FACT
The Big Duck really is big. It stands 20 feet tall and is an impressive 30 feet long.

## Big Duck

***Flanders, New York***

Conceived by "duck rancher" Martin Maurer and his wife, Jeule, as a means of selling the Peking ducks they raised, Long Island's Big Duck was built in Riverhead and relocated to Flanders in 1936. After development threatened the Big Duck in 1987, the owners donated the building to Suffolk County, and it was relocated to a park. In 2007, the Duck packed its bags once again and returned to its original site in Flanders where it now serves as a gift shop and tourist information center.

### All "Ducked" Out

Forget the tree! Folks in Suffolk County decorate the Big Duck for the holidays, festooning it with garland and lights. The town hosts an annual lighting ceremony to ring in the holiday season. We think that sounds just ducky!

## World's Largest Kaleidoscope

***Mount Tremper, New York***

You have to admire American ingenuity and the spirit that drives it. Only in this land of milk and honey could construction of the world's largest kaleidoscope seem so terribly vital. Lucky for us!

The Kaatskill Kaleidoscope at Emerson Place screams "fun" from the get-go. Housed in a converted grain silo, the 60-foot-tall world champ was originally jacketed in a sky-blue facade on which a strange set of eyes had been painted. Now it's shrouded in stealthy flat black.

Once inside the silo, which accommodates up to 20 people, visitors are treated to a ten-minute psychedelic slideshow featuring kaleidoscopic patterns. The images are seen via three reflective panels that project dazzling scenes 50 feet across the top of the silo.

Designed by Isaac Abrams, the giant kaleidoscope has stood in this Catskill Mountain Valley since 1996. The artist has ambitiously deemed his creation the "first cathedral of the third millennium." We can't speak to that, but the terms "groovy" and "far out" do spring to mind.

# Cardiff Giant

### *Cooperstown, New York*

It seems people will believe anything if they want to badly enough. Take for instance the Cardiff Giant, a ten-foot-tall petrified stone man "discovered" in 1869 on a farm in Cardiff, New York. Could the giant be the missing evolutionary link? Perhaps a visitor from another planet? Might he even have biblical implications? People wanted to know.

The answer, as it turns out, was none of the above. In reality, the Cardiff Giant was a divine hoax perpetrated by the farm's owner William C. "Stub" Newell and his pal George Hull. Concocted partly as a joke but also to turn a profit, the pair charged visitors fifty cents apiece to see the huge stone man up close. There were thousands of takers.

Eventually, the pranksters grew bored of the ruse and sold the giant to a group of businessmen for $37,500. Once the petrified man was placed on display at Syracuse, New York, a closer examination revealed the truth. Oddly, it didn't seem to matter. People were still fascinated by the giant and came out in droves to see "Old Hoaxey" in person. These days, the giant remains a major draw at the Farmers Museum in Cooperstown (home of the Baseball Hall of Fame), New York. Good show, big guy.

## Desert Storm Muffler Man

***Havre de Grace, Maryland***

The Muffler Men are at it again. This time we locate one in Havre de Grace, Maryland, an idyllic hamlet located at the confluence of the Susquehanna River and the Chesapeake Bay. This particular colossal character comes cloaked in desert fatigues—all the better if one wishes to fight a symbolic war for the good ol' USA.

Like others from his pituitary platoon, this specimen stands head and shoulders above mere mortals. Originally "employed" at the site as a service station attendant in the 1960s, the big fellow was "drafted" by current owner Ron Lynch of Lynch's Super Service in 1991 when America entered into Operation Desert Storm.

Since that time, the serviceman has endured rain, sleet, snow, and everything else Mother Nature could throw at him. In the new millennium, he was symbolically redeployed to Afghanistan and Iraq to assist his American compatriots.

## *The Awakening* Sculpture

### *National Harbor, Maryland*

In a classic bit of American weirdness, *The Awakening*, a 70-foot-long by 17-foot-high "screaming" sculpture by J. Seward Johnson, Jr., was moved from its Hains Point, Washington, D.C., home to Oxen Hill, Maryland, in 2008.

The aluminum behemoth whose wildly contorted facial expressions suggest a perpetually bad day, had struggled at Hains Point in his half-buried state since 1980, when it was created as part of a public art exhibition. Eventually, the sculpture was loaned to the National Park Service, which maintained stewardship of the statue until it was sold to billionaire developer Milton Peterson for the hefty price of $750,000. Peterson saw fit to provide the grumpy giant with new "digs" on a faux beach at National Harbor, Maryland—*the* playground for the upwardly mobile. Now, "power walkers" and chic restaurant patrons can catch a daily glimpse of the man who's clearly having a worse day than they. Progress!

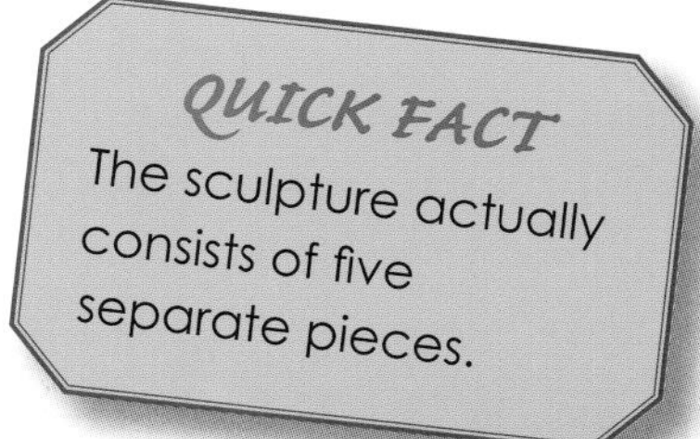

## God's Ark of Safety

***Frostburg, Maryland***

Faith is said to move mountains. It can also build arks. We could be referring to a famous ship commanded by a fellow named Noah. We are not. God's Ark of Safety is a modern incarnation of that biblical boat that totally skips the middleman. And it's made from steel!

In May 1974, Pastor Richard Green had a series of visions featuring a large ark on a hillside. Through these revelations, Green believes God asked him to build his new church as a replica of Noah's Ark. According to Green it would be a "sign to the world of God's love and the soon return of Jesus." The pastor complied. On Easter day in 1976, the first spade of dirt was turned, and God's Ark of Safety was underway.

More than three decades later, the ark stands as a rusting hulk less than half-finished. Faith may move mountains, but construction requires labor and money, each of which arrives in drips and drabs. When/if finished, the ark will measure an astounding 450 feet long by 75 feet wide.

Undaunted, the congregation meets each Sunday at a temporary church located beside the ark. Church members are certain that Pastor Green's vision will one day be realized. It has to be. After all, God himself commanded it.

*Progress on the ark* (above) *is slow. It may be some time before it resembles the finished product that designers have envisioned* (below).

### Searching for the Ark

Are the remains of Noah's Ark still out there? Christian groups have been searching for evidence of the Ark since the 1800s. The hunt has been centered on Mount Ararat based on a passage from Genesis.

## Grotto of Lourdes Replica

***Emmitsburg, Maryland***

**QUICK FACT**

The year 2008 marked the 150-year anniversary of Mary's apparitions at the Grotto of Lourdes in France.

If cash-strapped pilgrims can only dream of a journey to the Grotto of Lourdes in France, they're in for a treat. The National Shrine Grotto of Our Lady of Lourdes in Emmitsburg, Maryland, has brought the miracle to them.

When young Bernadette Soubiroux saw the Blessed Virgin Mary at a grotto in southern France in 1858, she caused quite a stir. Since then, people have flocked from all parts of the globe to experience the purported healing powers of the Grotto's spring at Lourdes.

The replica in Emmitsburg dates to 1875. It was established by Father John Dubois (founder of the adjacent Mount Saint Mary's College in 1808) with assistance from Saint Elizabeth Ann Seton (founder of the Sisters of Charity).

A meandering path encounters altars and chapels on its way to the "Grotto Cave," a close replica of the site where Soubiroux was said to receive her revelations. The grounds are of such uncommon beauty, secularists and people of other faiths may appreciate them at a level similar to their Christian counterparts. Such can be the beauty of faith.

## Little Jamaica

***Washington, D.C.***

Some people reserve a special place in their hearts for their native land. Case in point? Donald Morgan, a retired sociology professor from Maryland's Bowie State College. The transplanted Jamaican so missed his native country, he decided to reclaim it—right on his own front lawn.

Actually, this is only part of the story. In 1979, when Morgan built his enormous relief map of Jamaica, political turmoil between the island and the United States was at an all-time high. As a sociologist, Morgan knew that people warmed to things more readily if they understood them. With this thought in mind, Morgan got to work. One year later, "Mini-Jamaica" (our coining) was born.

So, what's featured here? About as much Jamaica as can be crammed in a 15- by 55-foot plot of land. There's Montego Bay, Cove Bay, and Morant Bay; a lump that's supposed to symbolize Blue Mountain (Jamaica's tallest peak); and, of course, a tribute to Bob Marley.

When Morgan's electric pump is functioning, there's even turbulent water lapping at Jamaica's shores.

## World Trade Center Memorial Replica

***Tinton Falls, New Jersey***

Some sculptures are abstract, some more literal. When 9/11 memorials popped up around New Jersey, most included the names of those lost that terrible day as well as a sketch or photograph of the Twin Towers as they once appeared. The town of Tinton Falls did things a bit differently. They erected a dead-ringer monument to the towers that's so very lifelike, it sends shivers down the spines of those who witnessed the tragedy firsthand.

The replica stands majestically on the front lawn of Tinton's firehouse. At eight feet high, the towers can't be mistaken for the real thing, yet compared with other monuments they are huge. While their size is intriguing, it's their attention to detail that really sets them apart.

The silver hue of their facade is historically correct, as is the antenna mast on the north tower. Some 40,000 drilled holes faithfully represent windows. There's even an "X" at the point where the airliners impacted each building.

But it's at night that the memorial turns downright eerie. This is when interior lights are flicked on and reality suddenly becomes fuzzy—particularly to those New Jerseyans who once viewed the twin towers from across the Hudson. If his goal was to keep people from forgetting, designer Jared Stevens has clearly done his job.

## Lucy the Elephant

***Margate, New Jersey***

There are elephants and there are *elephants.* Jumbo, the famous pachyderm that P. T. Barnum featured in the 1880s, was one enormous fellow. If we're to believe the famously deceptive showman, Jumbo was some 13 feet tall at the shoulder. In reality, he probably came closer to 11 feet. But even Jumbo in all of his magnificence paled in comparison with Lucy, the elephant from Margate.

Now, some may argue that Jumbo was a real living elephant, whereas Lucy is just a reproduction made from wood and tin. A mere technicality, we say. Besides, if one attempted to climb up into Jumbo's nether regions, that person would likely be trampled. Lucy not only allows such antics, she actually encourages them.

Built in 1881 by developer James V. Lafferty, Lucy was created as an attention-grabbing centerpiece that would put the former "South Atlantic City" on the map. At 65 feet tall by 60 feet long and weighing some 90 tons, Lucy was hard to miss.

Lucy is the only example of "zoomorphic architecture" left in the United States. Staircases in her legs lead to rooms inside. Over the years, Lucy has served as a summer home, tavern, and tourist attraction. Preservationists completed a loving restoration in 2000.

These days, tours of Lucy's cavernous "guts" are conducted daily, and most patrons emerge slack-jawed in appreciation. Lucy is considered the largest elephant on planet Earth. But there may be something about her that's even better. No one has to follow *this* elephant around with a shovel.

## SS *Atlantus*

### *Cape May, New Jersey*

When a joke fails, it's said to have gone over like a "lead balloon." The implication is obvious since a lead balloon can't float. With this in mind, one must wonder why President Wilson saw fit to commission a fleet of *concrete* ships during World War I.

Despite beliefs to the contrary, concrete ships really did float. The president approved the construction of 24 such vessels simply because the war effort had made steel scarce. Launched on December 5, 1918, the SS *Atlantus* would carry troops and transport coal until 1920, when she'd be deemed too heavy and would be retired to a salvage yard.

In March 1926, a plan was hatched. The 250-foot-long *Atlantus* would become a half-submerged ferry dock at Cape May, New Jersey. The ship was towed to its new site. Before a channel could be dug to firmly anchor it, a storm hit. The ship drifted and beached 150 feet off the coast where she rests to this very day. To some, the ship's a slowly decaying conversation piece; to others, she's a renowned New Jersey landmark. To all, she's the SS *Atlantus*, the ship that went over like a "lead balloon."

**QUICK FACT**
Although President Wilson commissioned 24 concrete ships, only 12 were built. The cost? A total of $50 million.

## Martian Landing Site

***Grover's Mill, New Jersey***

To say that American people were more gullible in 1938 is to totally miss the point. While it's true that Orson Welles scared the tar out of them with his infamous "War of the Worlds" radio broadcast—a transmission so realistic that many thought America was actually being invaded by little green men from Mars—it's also true that this was an era that predated television, instant news, satellites, and cell phones.

In those days, when a broadcaster issued a bulletin, people listened. To further escalate matters, Welles had craftily mixed genuine details into his attack scenario. There really was a Grover's Mill, New Jersey. When people heard that it had suddenly become a Martian ground zero, they understandably panicked.

To memorialize the unique event, the town of Grover's Mill has erected a monument at Van Nest Park, the very spot where the fictional spaceships were said to have landed. It depicts Welles behind his microphone and a petrified family huddled around the family radio, clinging to his every word.

Rather curiously, the nearby Grover's Mill Pond is colored an ethereal green. This likely stems from algae and other such organisms. Then again, if a Martian made a water landing, one might expect such a verdant hue. You don't suppose...?

**QUICK FACT**

The "War of the Worlds" radio broadcast was a Halloween special. It aired on October 30, 1938.

The Cafe of the Pink Turtle
Sombrero
RESTAURANT
MEXICO SHOP

Ready yourself for a taste of southern hospitality. Noted for its gentility, the chivalrous South is a peaceful place of long, lazy days and tranquil, romantic nights.

But it's also where adrenaline-fueled activities such as moonshine running and stock-car racing were born. This mild-to-wild combination makes its presence felt in the offbeat world as well. From the proper southern breeding and downright "quackiness" of the Peabody Ducks in Memphis, Tennessee, to the unabashed tackiness of South Carolina's South of the Border, you never knows which mode you'll stumble upon next.

Still, one thing is pretty much a given. After a hard day of hunting for the strange and unusual, innkeepers will make your night one to remember. "Y'all sit back and relax for a spell," your hosts will say in their trademark southern accent. The directive will come as music to your ears.

*South of the Border, Dillon, South Carolina*

## World's Oldest Edible Ham

***Smithfield, Virginia***

The man who brought Smithfield Ham to national prominence, P. D. Gwaltney, Jr., found his bosom buddy completely by accident. Sifting through his warehouse in 1922, he came across a 20-year-old ham that had miraculously escaped shipping. As a testament to his company's curing process, the ham appeared remarkably appetizing—even if it had lost some 65 percent of its original weight.

Recognizing the meatiness of the situation, the pork huckster quickly bolted into action. With the instincts of a showman and an eye on publicity, Gwaltney initially took out a $1,000 insurance policy on his newfound "friend." (The policy was increased to $5,000 after the ham was featured in *Ripley's* in 1932.) How long might his pet ham last, he wondered. He aimed to find out.

By most accounts, the unlikely duo were inseparable. Like a proud papa, Gwaltney would drag his prized ham to exhibitions, food fairs, get-togethers—anywhere ham-loving (buying?) people might gather. But even with this burden, Gwaltney never felt hamstrung. In fact, the two were only getting started.

In 1932, *Ripley's Believe It or Not* featured Gwaltney's pal as the World's Oldest Ham, an honor that would bring with it national recognition and separate it from scores of other "ham and eggers."

*P. D. Gwaltney, Jr., and Pet Ham*

*Courtesy of Isle of Wight County Museum, David Liebman*

Eventually, Gwaltney had a brass collar fitted to his slowly decaying pal. This served two purposes. First, it cleared up any doubt about ownership by proclaiming the petrified porker, "Mr. Gwaltney's Pet Ham." Second, it provided a way to chain his feted treasure to the ground.

For 14 long years the two pals moved happily about in gastronomic circles, until one awful day in 1936 when Gwaltney headed off to that big curing center in the sky. Would this tragic event signal the end of his beloved porker as well? "Not a HAM CHANCE!" fans seemed to say.

Happily rescued by the residents of Smithfield, Gwaltney's pride and joy would carry on. In 2002, the ham celebrated its 100th anniversary. In 2003, *Ripley's Believe it or Not* again honored Gwaltney's friend as the World's Oldest Ham.

Today, the porker seems as gamy as ever as it begs for notice at Smithfield's quaint Isle of Wight Museum. There, stored safely beneath protective glass, the storied ham rests beside a life-size cardboard cutout of its beloved master.

Occasionally, visitors observe wistful glances between Gwaltney and the ham as they ride out eternity, side by shank. For the sake of all that's strange, we can only hope these folks aren't lying. A man and his meat, such as it were, should never be trifled with.

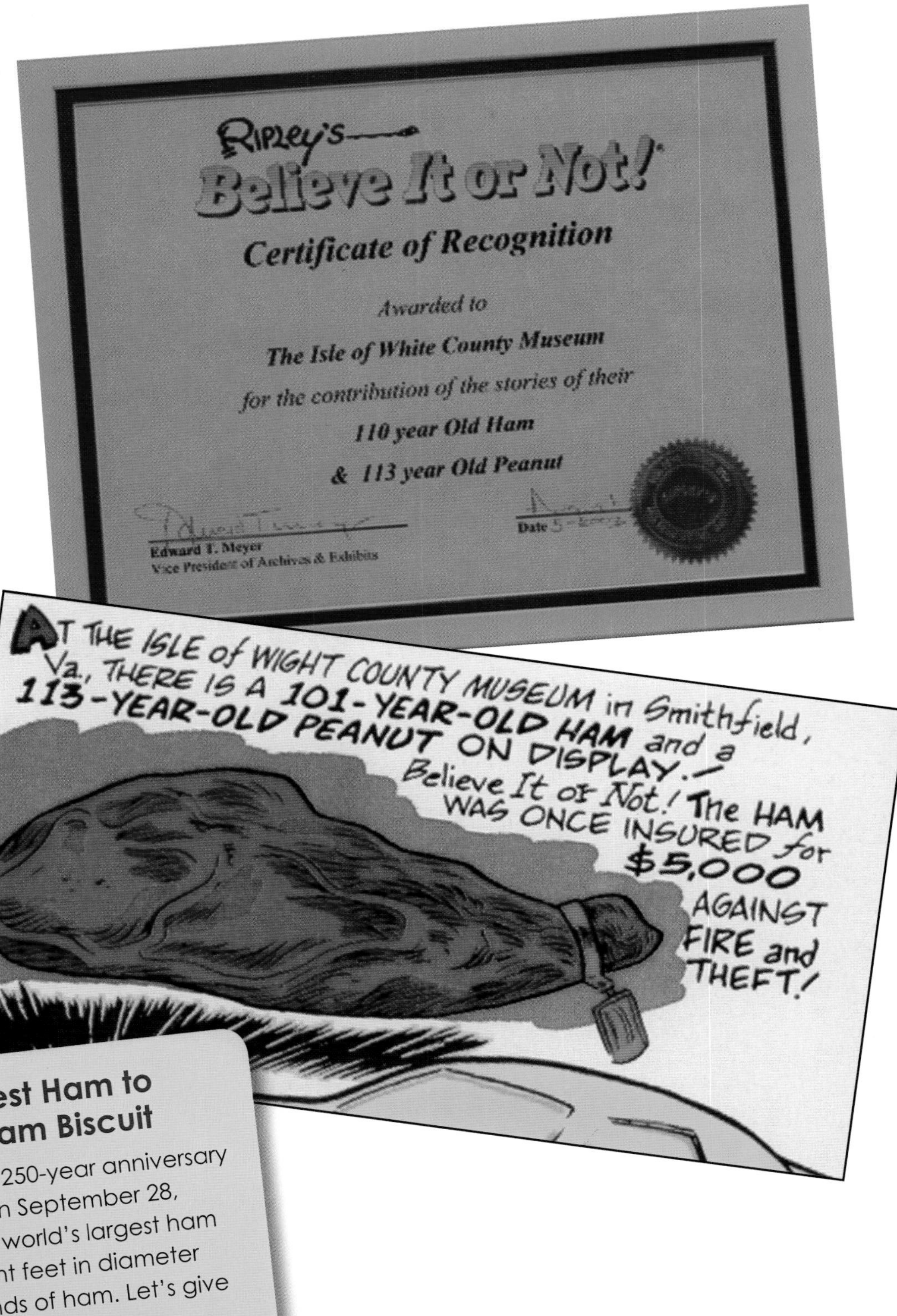


## From World's Oldest Ham to World's Largest Ham Biscuit

Smithfield commemorated its 250-year anniversary by hamming it up. Literally. On September 28, 2002, the town prepared the world's largest ham biscuit. The creation was eight feet in diameter and was piled with 500 pounds of ham. Let's give the "ham"let of Smithfield a hand!

## Flying Circus Airshow

***Bealeton, Virginia***

It's up, up, and away each Sunday (May through October) at Bealeton as old-time flyers relive the golden age of aviation. A weekly tradition that got off the ground in 1971, the Flying Circus Airshow features aerobatic maneuvers, wing walkers, sky-divers, formation flyers, and a multitude of winged pursuits.

The vintage aircraft recall barnstorming days and feature 1930s and 1940s Stear-man and Waco biplanes, as well as other open cockpit craft. If attendees wish to take to the wide, blue yonder, a cash fee will put them in the passenger seat. Not a bad deal for the rising Red Barons among us.

## Commodore Theater

***Portsmouth, Virginia***

Dinner theaters that combine food and a live stage show are fairly common, and it's easy to understand why. After all, what could be more fun than pairing entertainment with food? Portsmouth's Commodore Theater may have hit upon the answer to that particular question: a fine-dining restaurant coupled with a movie auditorium.

The restored 1945 Art Deco movie palace now features a modern 41- by 21-foot screen and full digital sound. But it wasn't always so. When rescued by present owner Fred Schoenfeld in 1987, the building had been vacant for nearly 12 years.

Originally designed to hold more than 1,000 moviegoers, the Commodore now seats 190 patrons in its dining area and 318 in its balcony. The dinner theater's menu features hearty American fare, soft drinks, and beer, as well as popcorn by the bucketful. One can only imagine the visceral thrill of slicing into a rare steak while watching a "slasher" movie.

**QUICK FACT**

The Commodore doesn't admit children under eight years of age.

## American Celebration on Parade

***Shenandoah Caverns, Virginia***

Earl Hargrove, Jr., had a dream. As the head honcho of a company that staged conventions and trade shows, the fanatical collector needed a space to house his beloved floats, props, and parade materials. His dream materialized when he purchased the Shenandoah Caverns attraction, which features a beautiful and unusual cavern and is open for tours. Hargrove erected a 40,000-square-foot building near the caverns intended strictly for the purpose of displaying his floats.

American Celebration on Parade's floats trace to past Thanksgiving parades, Miss America processions, even President Bill Clinton's 1996 inaugural parade. But parade floats represent only a portion of the collector's bounty. Visitors will also find truly wacky items such as a 30-foot-tall genie, a humongous puppy in a wagon, and an enormous American flag made from 5,000 square yards of crushed silk.

"People enjoy seeing the floats—how big they are, how complicated they are, and how well dressed out they are," Hargrove explains. "Our visitors get a sense that they are seeing a little bit of history here."

In addition to the floats, the museum contains an eclectic potpourri of items fairly begging for discovery. There's a parrot

### Say Cheese!

If you're looking for a photo op, look no further than American Celebration on Parade. Visitors are allowed to board a handful of floats to pose for photos.

overlooking an arctic scene that features a ferocious polar bear. Beside the bruin, a giant rabbit seeks out his next conquest. Pelicans, elephants, and a stuffed bison add to the mix.

When asked to name a favorite item at his vast repository, the patriotic man cuts right to the chase. "I guess it would be the American flag because we've had so many great experiences with it." No doubt.

## Prabhupada's Palace of Gold

***Moundsville, West Virginia***

*Opulence* is a word that's tossed about with abandon, but when it's truly deserved, there will be no doubt. Such is the case with Prabhupada's Palace of Gold. As its name implies, the palace, built as a "gift of love" by Hare Krishna devotees of Swami Srila Prabhupada, is lavishly laden with 22-karat gold.

Called "America's Taj Mahal" by the *New York Times*, the citadel has looked upon the West Virginia countryside since 1979. Constructed by monastic volunteers, its turrets, minarets, and marble-bedecked rooms personify beauty and show what can be accomplished when ordinary people gather together for a shining cause.

You might have to see this one to actually believe it. The Palace grounds feature a dazzling array of flowers and more than 100 fountains—not to mention the swan boat that graces its lake. Inside, you'll find ten elaborate marble rooms, including a 30-ton main dome with a 4,200-piece crystal ceiling. If that doesn't amaze you, maybe the 31 stained-glass windows will catch your eye?

## West Virginia State Penitentiary

***Moundsville, West Virginia***

This fortresslike facility, which opened in 1876 and closed in 1995, is a throwback to "retribution" prisons. Here, under deplorable conditions in claustrophobic five- by seven-foot cells, emphasis was placed on punishment, not rehabilitation.

Today, tours lead "prisoners" past such areas as the Wagon Gate, a portion of the prison that features a trap door responsible for 85 hangings, and the North Hall, where the prison's most unruly spent 22 hours of each day in seclusion.

In addition to its harsh history, the prison is said to be haunted. A midnight tour provides visitors with a 90-minute overview of the place, then allows them to roam unaided until 6:00 A.M. This spookfest is the penitentiary's most popular tour.

**QUICK FACT**

The West Virginia State Penitentiary was the second public building established in the new state after the Civil War. We wonder what the first public building was. Grocery store, maybe?

## Home of the Mothman

***Point Pleasant, West Virginia***

Legend has it that from 1966 to 1967, the town of Point Pleasant was terrorized by a mysterious, shrieking winged creature. The figure most closely resembled a moth with humanlike features and stood between six and seven feet tall, with featherless wings and red eyes. Local lore indicated that dozens of townspeople had encounters with the mothlike creature before a 1967 bridge collapse (which the Mothman is said to have predicted) that resulted in the deaths of 46 people.

Today, the town pays homage to this tall, dark stranger with a 12-foot-tall stainless-steel sculpture and the world's only Mothman Museum. A yearly Mothman festival takes place every September.

**QUICK FACT**

*The Mothman Prophecies*, a book by journalist John Keel, documents the story of this fearsome creature with firsthand accounts from people who reportedly saw it. The book was later turned into a 2002 film of the same name starring Richard Gere.

## Philippi Mummies

***Philippi, West Virginia***

If you were entrusted with the preservation of 120-year-old mummies, would you store them in: A) A museum? B) A train depot? C) A restroom? D) All of the above? If you answered "D" you may already know about the Philippi Mummies. If not, read on.

In 1888, self-appointed scientist Graham Hamrick purchased two female cadavers from the West Virginia Hospital for the Insane. His plan? To re-create embalming techniques used by the ancient pharaohs. Whatever method Hamrick employed, it apparently worked. Today, the ladies appear fairly well-preserved—if a bit stone-faced.

The mummies traveled a convoluted path from there. They reportedly did the European circus act with P. T. Barnum, were misplaced for a few decades, spent time in a barn, and eventually ended up in the home of a local citizen. A severe flood relocated them to the front lawn of the town's post office, after which they were dried out and tended to.

Today, the rigid ladies are housed in the Barbour County Historical Museum at the former B & O Railroad Station in what used to be a bathroom. Does it get any weirder than this? You'll have to read on to see!

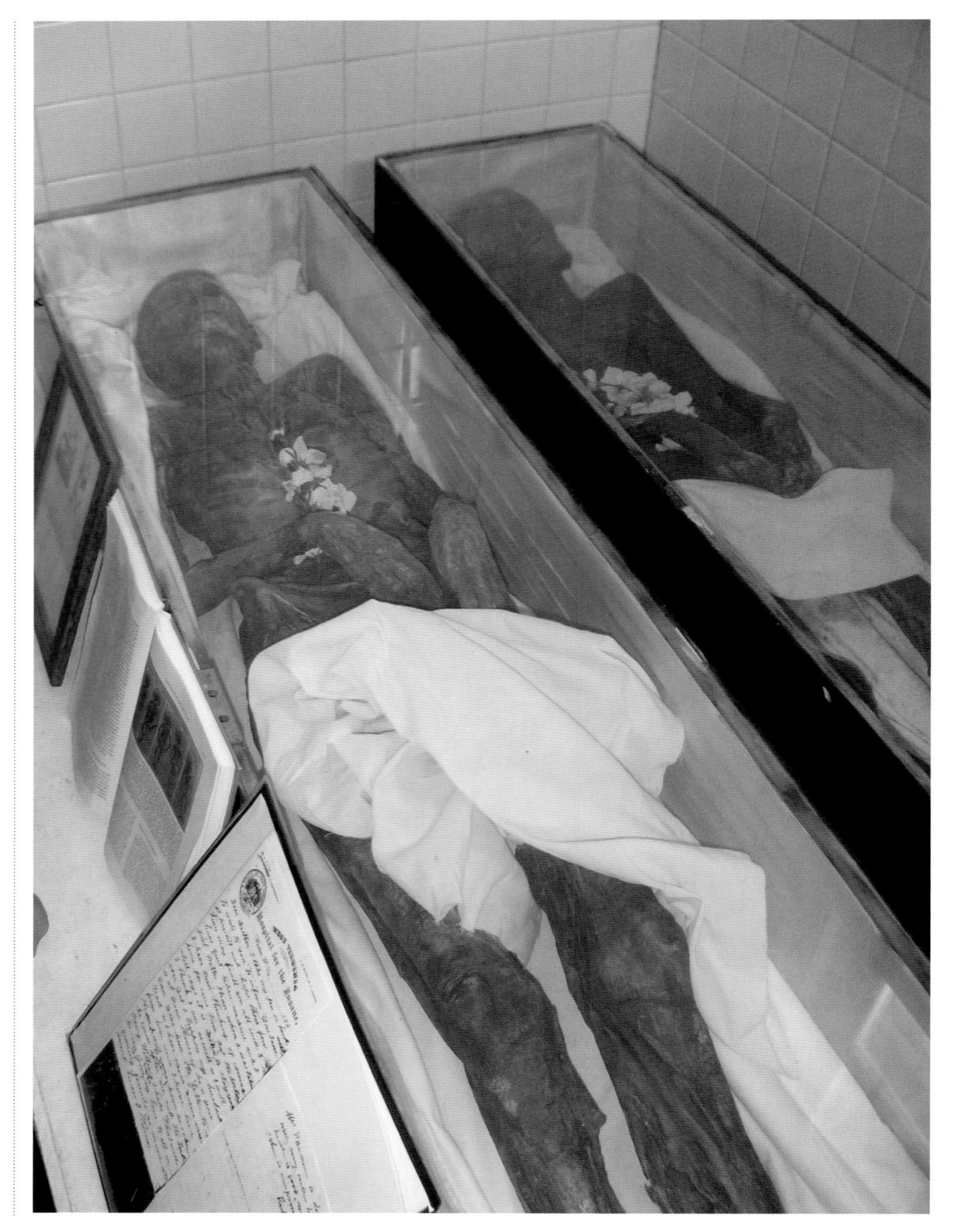

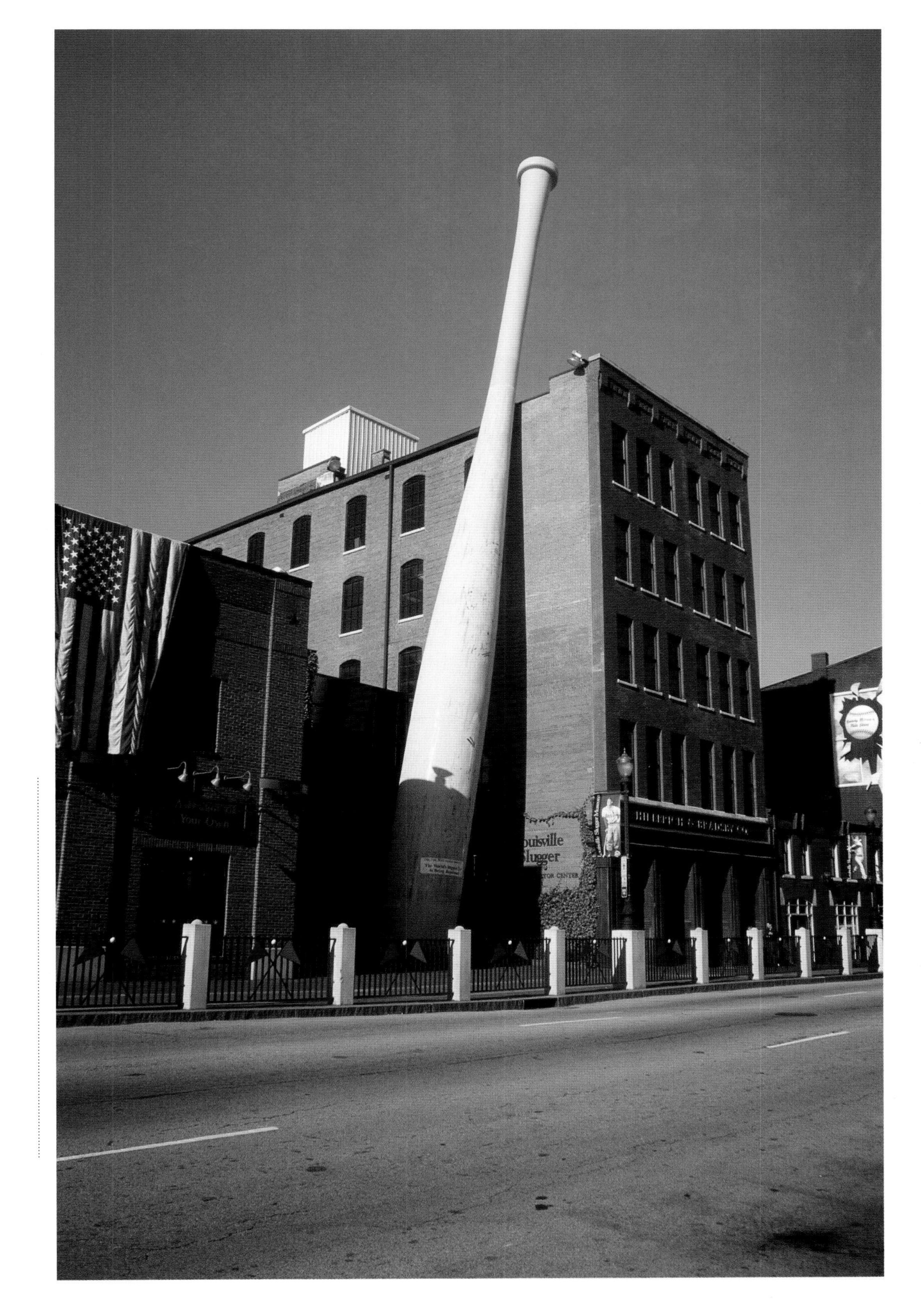

QUICK FACT
The factory produces approximately one million bats a year.

## World's Largest Baseball Bat

***Louisville, Kentucky***

Leaning against the Louisville Slugger Museum & Factory is a bat that has no equal, measuring 120 feet from tip to tip and weighing in at 34 tons. The steel bat is a scale replica of Babe Ruth's 34-inch Slugger. Close at hand are the World's Largest Baseball and the World's Largest Baseball Glove. Batter up!

## Lost River Cave

***Bowling Green, Kentucky***

Why trudge through a cave when you can glide across it in a boat? Bowling Green's Lost River Cave prides itself on offering the only underground boat tour in the state—and it's easy to see the attraction.

As one of a handful of watered cave systems in America, Lost River Cave features an agreeable river walk leading to one of the largest cave entrances east of the Mississippi River. From there, visitors can embark upon a 25-minute underground boat ride.

*Ripley's Believe It or Not* categorizes the Lost River as the shortest and deepest river in the world. If that doesn't impress you, maybe this will: The inimitable Jesse James and his gang are said to have visited the cave. Who could blame them? With all their tiresome running, the desperados probably fancied a cruise.

## Cumberland Falls Moonbow

***Corbin, Kentucky***

A *moonbow* is the nighttime equivalent of a rainbow. The major difference? A moonbow uses lunar, not solar, rays to produce the colorful phenomenon.

At 68 feet tall and 125 feet wide, Cumberland Falls has been dubbed "Little Niagara" by waterfall buffs. On nights featuring a full moon, the elusive moonbow sometimes appears. The event relies on a number of variables, including proper water temperature, agreeable mist cloud, and clear skies, but when the moonbow does appear, it's pure magic. The phenomenon is so popular, Web sites regularly track "optimal moonbow dates" so aficionados won't miss out.

## Cave City

***Cave City, Kentucky***

*Meet and greet ferocious dinosaurs at Cave City's Dinosaur World.*

If you are enticed by terms like "world's biggest" and "world's hokiest," you'll definitely want to plan a visit to Cave City. This offering in south-central Kentucky's cave country is locked in a glorious time warp of 1950s-era roadside fun and adventure.

First and foremost, the town owes its lifeblood to a giant hole in the ground. In a world of braggadocio, Mammoth Cave should win an award for truth in advertising. With more than 350 miles of passages discovered thus far, the 379-foot-deep cave system is considered the world's longest by a healthy margin. Each day, tourists arrive in throngs to explore its famed passageways and eat in its underground "Snowball Dining Room." But Mammoth Cave is merely the main lure to Cave City. There are many strange and unusual bits lurking about its periphery.

Take Dinosaur World, for example. With more than 100 full-size dinosaur statues arranged in a jungle setting, the attraction offers visitors a chance to meet these prehistoric giants personally. If that doesn't suit your fancy, the site also offers kids the opportunity to search for their very own fossils—which they can keep!

Guntown Mountain, another exercise in kitsch, features the time-honored Old West theme. This offering adds a touch of questionable authenticity to the genre, since Jesse James was thought to have hidden out in area caves. Gunfights and high-living abound.

By the way, Cave City is not called Cave City solely for Mammoth Cave. The geology that produced the giant has populated the area with a number of underground chambers.

When it's time to batten down the hatches and retire from spelunking, archeology, and gunfights, the Wigwam Village Inn is the perfect place to put one's 1950s roadside trip to bed. Literally.

*Wigwam Village Inn offers travelers an unusual place to spend the night.*

*More than just a big hole in the ground, Mammoth Cave delights and amazes visitors with its geological features.*

*This cave system is believed to be the longest in the world.*

## Harland Sanders Café and Museum

***Corbin, Kentucky***

**QUICK FACT**

Colonel Sanders wasn't really a colonel—at least not in the true sense of the word. The honorary title was bestowed upon him by the governor of Kentucky in 1935.

Long before Colonel Sanders sold his "finger-lickin' good" chicken from a chain of Kentucky Fried Chicken franchises, he stirred the pot here at his first store.

Actually, "store" is an overstatement. In 1930, the white-bearded Sanders operated a service station with a small six-seat lunchroom attached. In short order (pun intended), word spread about his uncommonly tasty fried chicken.

In 1937, Sanders enlarged his enterprise and built Sanders Café, a restaurant with accommodations for 142 customers. Kentucky Fried Chicken was on its way to fast-food superstardom.

Today, the restored Harland Sanders Café stands as the "Birthplace of Kentucky Fried Chicken." Next door, a modern KFC restaurant wows hungry patrons with its super-secret "11 herbs and spices." Yum!

### World Chicken Festival

Kentucky pays homage to Colonel Sanders through its annual World Chicken Festival, which takes place in London, Kentucky, every September. The festival features the World's Largest Stainless-steel Skillet—10 feet, 6 inches in diameter and 8 inches deep, with an 8-foot handle. The skillet weighs a whopping 700 pounds! Visitors to the festival can purchase chicken fried in this sizable skillet, which can cook 600 quarters of chicken at once. Anyone want seconds? How about thirds?

QUICK FACT

The Paris, Tennessee, replica consists of 500 pieces of Douglas fir, 6,000 steel rods, and 10,000 hours of volunteer labor.

## Eiffel Tower

***Paris, Tennessee***

If a town is named Paris and its inhabitants swim in civic pride, what's the next logical step? They build a replica of the Eiffel Tower to cement their association with the European land of brie and chardonnay.

In this case, the replica is vastly shorter than the original (70 feet versus 986 feet), but who's counting? It features most every metal bit that the original does and is even painted a similar hue.

The tower was originally created at Christian Brothers University in Memphis, Tennessee, and was initially some ten feet shorter. However, when citizens of Paris, Tennessee, learned that Paris, Texas, had built a 65-foot replica, they pushed their pinnacle to 70 feet. *Viva la difference!*

## The Peabody Ducks

***Memphis, Tennessee***

If it walks like a duck and quacks like a duck, it must be a duck, right? Not if it's a *Peabody* duck from the esteemed troupe of marching ducks at the Peabody Hotel. To call one of these thoroughbreds by such a pedestrian name is akin to confusing opera with pop music.

The grand tradition began in 1933 when prankster and general manager Frank Schutt put three live ducks in the hotel's fountain as a joke. Guests loved the sight so much the hotel replaced the three original ducks with five Mallard ducks.

In 1940, bellman and former circus animal trainer Edward Pembroke offered to assist in duck duties and eventually taught the ducks to march. He became the official Peabody "Duckmaster" and remained in that capacity until 1991.

Seven decades later, the "quackers" are still moving in lockstep. Here's the drill: Every day at 11:00 A.M., the ducks are led by their duckmaster to the Peabody Grand Lobby. A red carpet is unfurled, and the ducks commence marching to the tune of John Philip Sousa's *King Cotton March*. At 5:00 P.M., the ceremony is reversed, and the cultured ducks retreat to their penthouse lair for the evening.

Surprisingly, the regal birds don't live the uppity life for very long. Every three months, a new team is trained, and the veterans are returned to farms to live out their lives. This must be pretty hard on the quackers. Would you want to dine on farm muck after you'd sampled beef Wellington?

**QUICK FACT**
The March of the Peabody Ducks is also performed at the Peabody hotels in Little Rock, Arkansas, and Orlando, Florida.

PEABODY

# Salt and Pepper Shaker Museum

***Gatlinburg, Tennessee***

Proving that no object is too ordinary to build a museum around, this shrine to salt and pepper shakers is one woman's spicy dream come true.

Owner Andrea Ludden is a trained archeologist who hails from Belgium. She has managed to collect more than 20,000 salt and pepper shakers, which she houses in fastidious order in her multiroom museum in Gatlinburg. Already the venue is packed to overflowing. It's not the first time Ludden has run out of space.

After building her collection for more than two decades, Ludden first opened a museum in Cosby, Tennessee. That building proved too small for her ever-burgeoning inventory, and she was forced to relocate. She moved to her present space in 2004, but history may repeat itself since Ludden's collecting bug shows no sign of abating.

Ludden's salt and pepper shakers come from everywhere and anywhere and are made from glass, plastic, wood, metal, crystal, walnut shells, seashells, nuts, eggs—the list goes on.

There are shakers shaped like ears of corn, tractors, apples, gumball machines, log cabins, people, places, animals—if it can be imagined, it was probably manufactured.

In addition, there are shakers that celebrate pop culture, with the Beatles heading up the British invasion, and shakers that question good "taste," such as replicas of the human foot and toilet offerings.

Will Andrea Ludden's enterprise outgrow its present home and force her to relocate once again? If things shake out the way we think they will, it's almost a certainty. We don't suppose Ludden would want it any other way.

## Parthenon

***Nashville, Tennessee***

Anyone who claims to see the Greek goddess Athena while standing beside Nashville's Parthenon should be excused. They are *not* dreaming. In keeping with their "Athens of the South" nickname, the city of Nashville chose to build this full-scale replica for the Tennessee Centennial Exposition in 1897.

Originally constructed of wood, plaster, and brick, Nashville's Parthenon was rebuilt out of concrete in the 1920s. If it were placed side by side with its Greek counterpart, it's actually *more* faithful to the original design, since the ravages of time have not yet taken their toll.

Today, the Parthenon operates as an art gallery and is a well-known landmark in Centennial Park. In 1990, a 41-foot, 10-inch statue of Athena Parthenos was added. Artist Alan LeQuire's work faithfully replicates Athens' long-lost sculpture.

QUICK FACT

The Athena Parthenos statue holds a unique honor—it's the tallest indoor statue in the Western world.

## Shell-Shape Filling Station

***Winston-Salem, North Carolina***

Built in 1930 by the Quality Oil Company (a local Shell Oil marketer), this shell-shape station made it clear to gas-thirsty visitors what brand of dino-juice it pumped. Originally one of eight such "scallops" in the Winston-Salem area, this station stands as the sole survivor.

After its gas-pumping days had passed, the station enjoyed a second life as a lawn-mower repair shop. But by the late 1990s, it had fallen into disrepair.

Today, the bright yellow building is spiffier than new, and two old-time pumps (donated by Shell Oil) appear ready to "fill 'er up." But alas, it's just a pretty facade. In reality, this primo example of novelty architecture serves as a satellite office for Preservation North Carolina.

**QUICK FACT**

Preservation North Carolina spent $50,000 to restore the station to its former glory.

## World's Largest Chest of Drawers

***High Point, North Carolina***

Originally known as the "Bureau of Information," High Point's big chest of drawers was constructed as a monument to the city's status as "Home Furnishings Capital of the World." The chest is actually the facade of a building—the home of the High Point Jaycees (a humanitarian organization).

**QUICK FACT**

Need to purchase a chest of drawers of your own? You can't go wrong in High Point. You'll find more than 50 furniture stores here.

# Devil's Tramping Ground

***Siler City, North Carolina***

What would you call a 40-foot barren circle, situated in the middle of a productive forest, that hasn't grown so much as a weed for hundreds of years? North Carolinians call it the Devil's Tramping Ground.

Since the Department of Agriculture can't explain the phenomenon, dark theories abound. These include extraterrestrial visits and appearances by the devil himself.

A more down-to-earth explanation involves a particularly high salt level in the soil. Still, this doesn't account for the Tramping Ground's near perfect circular shape.

Another nod to the occult comes by way of firsthand reports that objects placed in the circle overnight will vanish by morning, never to be found again.

In 1949, journalist John William Harden (1903–1985) added to the legend when he wrote:

"The Devils Tramping Ground, the Chatham natives say... There, sometimes during the dark of night the Majesty of the Underworld of Evil silently tramps around that bare circle—thinking, plotting, and planning against the god, and in behalf of wrong. So far as is known no person has ever spent the night there to disprove this is what happens."

Any volunteers?

## South of the Border

***Dillon, South Carolina***

It seems some of the greatest places have billboards that sing their praises from hundreds of mile away. (See Wall Drug, page 194). In this case, that place is called South of the Border. Despite its Mexican pretensions, this classic tourist attraction is *not* positioned south of the border unless, of course, one is referring to the borderline of North and South Carolina.

South of the Border is located on I-95, just below the North Carolina line in Dillon, South Carolina. This location, not coincidentally, is the approximate halfway point to Florida for drivers making the trek out of New York. The ever-crafty Pedro, the lovable mascot of South of the Border, realized that drivers might be a bit road-weary at this point and set out to right this eminent wrong. Boy, did he succeed!

The earliest taste of Pedro arrives some 200 miles out when the first of the establishment's many billboards are encountered. Travelers begin to wonder what all the hoopla is about as they drive past signs with clever cracks like, "Pedro's Weather Forecast: Chili Today, Hot Tamale" and "You Never Sausage a Place! You're Always a Weiner at Pedro's!" If they're making the ride at night, a virtual explosion of light will let tired motorists know when they've finally arrived.

Sticking out like a gaudy piñata, the 200-foot-tall neon sombrero welcomes visitors. Nearby is a 97-foot-tall neon Pedro figure so enormous that cars can drive through his legs. Within this "Mexican" city, visitors will find over-the-top restaurants, motels, fireworks vendors, souvenir stands, an RV park—even a chapel that performs real weddings.

Visitors who ascend the sombrero tower quickly realize that this funky-fun oasis of activity exists in a region of near nothingness. All thanks to Pedro.

**Going Up?**

The neon sombrero that welcomes visitors to South of the Border also affords them a view. A glass elevator in the center of the sombrero shoots guests 200 feet up to the top of Sombrero Tower.

# World's Largest Fire Hydrant: Busted Plug Plaza

***Columbia, South Carolina***

The artist known as Blue Sky—born Warren Edward Johnson—spearheaded the design, construction, and installation of this four-story sculpture. Located in a downtown bank's parking lot, the metallic hydrant is "busted" in that it doubles as a fountain, pumping water in and out of a surrounding pool 24 hours a day. While other contenders claim to be the world's largest hydrant, Sky's creation—durable enough to withstand a direct hit by a tornado—is the undisputed champ.

**QUICK FACT**

The sculpture weighs 675,000 pounds, and construction took 14 months.

## Pink and Gray Elephants

***Hardeeville, South Carolina***

These life-size fiberglass pachyderms stand sentry at Papa Joe's Fireworks near I-95, giving the establishment a trunk up on the competition. While fireworks are sold year-round in Hardeeville, it is illegal to light them within city limits all but two days of the year: New Year's Day and the Fourth of July.

## Jimmy Carter Peanut

***Plains, Georgia***

To honor our peanut-producing past president (try saying that three times fast), a mighty peanut stands proud in Jimmy Carter's hometown of Plains, Georgia. Built by Indiana residents James Kiely, Doyle Kifer, and Loretta Townsend, the 13-foot-tall peanut originally oversaw a 1976 campaign visit to Evanston, Indiana. After the ceremonies, the big nut was shipped off to Plains.

The peanut, flaunting a toothy smile that could only come from Carter's happy kisser, suffered great indignities over time. While it was berthed at the Plains train depot, the peanut was nearly gouged to pieces by nutty souvenir hunters; yearly wear and tear also took its toll.

Thankfully, the local Davis E-Z Shop stepped in, filled the peanut's bottom with concrete, and anchored it down in front of their store. Successive repairs have rendered it good enough to eat.

## World's Largest Peanut

***Ashburn, Georgia***

To verify this legume's grand claim, we may need a ruling from the judges. Touted as the World's Largest Peanut, this specimen measures in at a comparatively *underwhelming* ten feet tall. The Jimmy Carter Peanut in Plains, Georgia, easily outshells it at 13 feet. On the other hand, the World's "Largest" Peanut *is* perched atop a 15-foot-tall brick column.

Erected in 1975, the peanut rests on top of a crown that reads "1st in Peanuts." Since Georgia's main crop is peanuts, and the world's largest processing plant is located in Ashburn, this sounds reasonable. Nevertheless, we'd be nuts to award this peanut top honors without something a bit more definitive!

## Trash Statue of Liberty

***McRae, Georgia***

In 1986, the local Lions Club undertook the building of a second Lady Liberty. This was done to commemorate the original green lady's 100th anniversary and to remind people of America's true purpose.

With nothing more than pieces of old Styrofoam, a tree stump, and other discarded materials, they erected a one-twelfth scale "trash" Statue of Liberty that closely approximates the original.

The "artists" used old photos for cues as they went along, but perhaps their picture of the base was somewhat lacking. For whatever reason, the replica tapers toward the top (like the original) then grows wide again just before the statue is reached (decidedly *unlike* the original). Can you say "artistic license"?

**QUICK FACT**

France gave the real Statue of Liberty to the United States as a gift in 1886.

## Pope, Dickson, and Son Funeral Home and Museum of Funeral Memorabilia

***Jonesboro, Georgia***

Funeral home owner Abb Dickson must have a playful spirit. Installing a small museum behind his funeral parlor, Dickson thoughtfully included a large window that opens to the parking lot. This permits "viewing" from inside one's car. If a patron came here for sad reasons, as most probably do, they'd effectively get two viewings in the same day.

The museum features a horse-drawn hearse once employed to transport Alexander H. Stephens, the vice president of the Confederacy; a small Civil War–issue iron casket, used to ship deceased young boys home for burial; and other funeral memorabilia.

A multifaceted funeral home "resting" on the cutting edge? That's Pope, Dickson, and Son!

## Babyland General Hospital

***Cleveland, Georgia***

Who could forget the Cabbage Patch Kid craze of the early 1980s? For parents of young daughters, obtaining one of these moppets became a mission second only to guarding their child's life. While the fad has died down, the dolls still continue to sell.

Like all offspring, the Cabbage Patch Kids hail from somewhere. Legend has it that they arrive not by stork but via the Babyland General "Hospital," located in the mountains of northern Georgia.

Creator Xavier Roberts began producing the dolls in his homeland of Cleveland, Georgia, in 1978. Originally marketed as "Little People," the dolls were said to have emerged from a cabbage patch. Eventually, a name change to Cabbage Patch would attest to their lineage and earn them a place in toy-making history.

Today, the hospital/factory continues to attract tourists. Visitors can watch dolls being "born" in the cabbage patch and observe the cutie-pies as they attend school. To complete the picture, all staff members wear crisp white doctors' or nurses' uniforms.

## Lunchbox Museum
### *Columbus, Georgia*

Children from a not-too-distant era happily carried lunchboxes to school. These lightweight metal containers, emblazoned with the names and pictures of popular television shows, heartthrobs, cowboy heroes, and the like kept kids' lunches safe and secure. They were as individual as each child and favored by most.

Alan Woodall has tapped into this past craze with a vast collection of colorful lunch houses. Billed as the "World's Largest Lunchbox Museum," Woodall's collection at the Rivermarket Antique Mall numbers in the thousands and shows no sign of letting up.

Visitors to the museum can feast their eyes upon such lunchbox favorites as Hopalong Cassidy, David Cassidy, Daniel Boone, Bonanza, Flipper, Charlie's Angels, Bobby Sherman, Superman, the Dukes of Hazzard, Mickey Mouse, and literally thousands of others. If the subject matter held some form of popularity during the 1950s through 1960s, chances are good that a lunchbox paid it homage.

Thermoses and coolers round out the collection and bring back happy memories to more than a few.

For those wondering why lunchboxes finally rode off into the sunset, the owner points directly at the Florida legislature. In 1972, they ruled that each metal lunchbox should be viewed as a "lethal weapon." Funny, we thought that was a movie. In fact, we think a Mel Gibson/Danny Glover lunchbox would be fat city.

## U.S. National Tick Collection

***Statesboro, Georgia***

Just when you think you've seen it all, the U.S. National Tick Collection (USNTC) repository comes along. The Statesboro facility houses 850 different species and more than one million specimens of ticks. Researchers study the parasites, hoping to gather the good and bad from each, but the USNTC isn't *all* business. One day each week, the facility conducts tours and educates the public on the profound differences between each species. Microscopes get visitors up close and personal with each tick.

Owned by the Smithsonian Institution, the enterprise features ticks that tick us off, such as those responsible for Lyme disease and Rocky Mountain Spotted Fever, as well as agreeable ones that show promise within the medical realm. Think of the USNTC as a zoo for bloodsuckers.

**QUICK FACT**

The USNTC houses the largest collection of ticks in the world.

## Providence Canyon State Park

***Stewart County, Georgia***

Providence Canyon has been dubbed Georgia's "Little Grand Canyon"—and for good reason. Peering up at its walls from the valley floor, visitors are treated to a striking array of orange, red, pink, and purple hues, similar to those found at the famous Arizona canyon. In reality, however, soft canyon soil, rather than element-weathered rock, provides this tapestry of colors.

The 150-foot-deep canyon encompasses more than 1,100 acres. It was formed by erosion after settlers clear-cut the land in the 1800s. In the 1930s, the Civilian Conservation Corp planted trees and plants in an effort to slow the process. In 1971, the unique area became a state park.

Despite its unlikely roots, the park provides breathtaking vistas, numerous hiking trails, fossilized areas, and a chance to commune with nature.

# World's Largest Bas-Relief Carving

***Stone Mountain, Georgia***

Stone Mountain, Georgia, is famous for a number of reasons, not the least of which is its unique appearance. As one of the world's largest exposed chunks of granite, the stone heap rears up from its flattish plateau much like Australia's Ayers Rock. But unique geology only scratches the surface of this mountain's appeal. There are three notable things about the imposing granite dome that separate it from all others: Confederate President Jefferson Davis, General Robert E. Lee, and Lieutenant-General Thomas "Stonewall" Jackson.

Geologists believe that Stone Mountain came into being during the Alleghenian Orogeny, a massive collision of tectonic plates that occurred about 350 million years ago.

At 1,683 feet above sea level, the mountain rises 825 feet from its base and covers some 583 acres. The fact that its just 16 miles from the megalopolis of Atlanta only adds to its allure.

No doubt sensing Stone Mountain's "wow" factor, in 1909, Helen Plane, chapter president of the United Daughters of the Confederacy, suggested that a relief carving of Robert E. Lee be created on the mountain's north face. After a succession of artists (including Gutzon Borglum, who would later carve Mount Rushmore), a number of fitful starts, and design changes, the carvings would finally be dedicated in 1970.

The engraved portion of the mountain covers more than three acres—an area larger than a football field. The rectangular frame that contains the historical figures measures 90 feet by 190 feet and is recessed 42 feet into the mountain. This makes it the world's largest bas-relief carving.

Today, people ride cable cars or trudge up a steep trail to reach the mountain's summit.

## Twistee Treat

***Florida (various locations)***

Another fine example of form meeting function is the Twistee Treat chain of ice cream shops that dot the Florida roadside, as well as a few select roadsides in the Midwest. The original company began building these 22-foot-tall cones (with retro 1950s-style interiors) in 1980 but went bankrupt a decade later. In 1996, a new Twistee Treat corporation emerged and is now in expansion mode once again.

## *Christ of the Abyss*

**Key Largo, Florida**

Should spiritual beliefs be neglected in the underwater realm? Italian sculptor Guido Galletti answers with a resounding "no." His *Christ of the Abyss* statue in Key Largo's Pennekamp Park (a.k.a. Key Largo Coral Reef Preserve) has attracted scuba divers and snorkelers from around the world since 1966.

The bronze statue is eight-and-a-half feet tall and is anchored to a 4,000-pound base that is situated some 25 feet below the ocean's surface. To reach it, visitors must take a three-mile boat ride from Key Largo. From there, it is necessary to snorkel or scuba dive to get a close look at the statue.

The statue is actually a cast of a 1954 forerunner placed underwater in the Mediterranean Sea near Genoa, Italy. The original piece, *Il Cristo Degli Abissi*, translates to *Christ of the Abyss*.

## Coral Castle

### *Homestead, Florida*

Homestead is known for its Coral Castle—a miraculous construction created by a mysterious man named Edward Leedskalnin (1887–1951).

The chief difference between Edward Leedskalnin's castle and other single-builder fortresses lies in its building materials. Coral Castle is built of huge coral blocks, some weighing as much as 30 tons. How Leedskalnin moved these into place, completely by himself and using early 1900s technology, has been equated with the mystery of the Great Pyramids. Some stones at Coral Castle weigh twice as much as the ones used at the Pyramids of Giza. How could one man possibly move these into place? For the record, Leedskalnin was about five feet tall and tipped the scales at an underwhelming 100 pounds.

Mind-boggling features can be found everywhere at the castle. A raised obelisk weighs a whopping 28 tons. A wall surrounding the palace stands eight feet tall and also pushes the scale into the multiple tons. A nine-ton swinging gate is balanced so precisely, the touch of a finger sets it into motion. Talk about engineering savvy!

Leedskalnin, a Latvian immigrant, began his project in 1920 and continued his efforts through 1940. Almost inexplicably, no one is reported to have witnessed the one-man building dynamo as he quarried, fashioned, and ultimately moved his huge coral stones into place. The belief that Leedskalnin worked primarily at night is indicative of his secretiveness and adds to the mysterious aura of the castle.

With no hard facts upon which to draw, theories concerning the construction abound. Some say Leedskalnin levitated the blocks using ethereal powers. Others say the diminutive man unlocked the secrets of antigravity. For his part, Leedskalnin was an outspoken believer in the power of magnetic current and suggested that this was responsible for his Coral Castle.

Could this scientific phenomenon be the driving force behind Coral Castle? Only Edward Leedskalnin knows for sure, and that information was buried with him in 1951.

**QUICK FACT**

Many may also remember Homestead, Florida, for a "big wind" named Andrew. In 1992, the Category 5 hurricane nearly obliterated this southern Florida town and forever ingrained its name in the annals of disaster history.

## Jules' Undersea Lodge

***Key Largo, Florida***

As its descriptive name implies, Jules' Undersea Lodge is located *undersea*. If this sounds just a trifle deadly, don't worry. The Lodge (named for science-fiction writer Jules Verne) is accessible to folks who use scuba gear. This includes seasoned sport divers as well as beginners.

The dive drill is simple. Descend 21 feet to the lodge and enter by swimming up into the "wet" room. Remove your gear and kick back. Like any modern lodge, air-conditioning, hot showers, music, and television await.

When the hunger gong sounds, a fully stocked galley provides caloric comfort. These lures, coupled with this unique environment, have snared some famous guests. Canadian Prime Minister Pierre Trudeau has taken the plunge, as have rockers Steven Tyler from Aerosmith, and—quite fittingly—Jon Fishman from Phish.

The brainchild of ocean researchers Neil Monney and Ian Koblick, the underwater motel might not be situated "20,000 Leagues Under the Sea" as Verne envisioned it, but it is *under* the sea. That's got to count for something!

**Do You Deliver?**

Hungry guests of the Lodge can actually order a pizza and have it delivered underwater. That's what we call service!

**QUICK FACT**

The Jules' Undersea Lodge didn't start off as a hotel. It was originally used as an underwater research facility.

## Skunk Ape Research Headquarters

***Ochopee, Florida***

Glomming onto the Bigfoot craze, the elusive Skunk Ape makes an appearance. Rarely, that is. For better than a half-century, the seven-foot-tall, frightfully hairy creature is said to have roamed and terrorized the hinterlands of South Florida.

Scientists doubt the creature's existence, as scientists usually do when it comes to such fantastic things. But that hasn't stopped Dave Shealy, a self-appointed expert in everything Skunk Ape.

As cofounder of the Skunk Ape Research Headquarters, Shealy, along with his brother, Jack, attempts to enlighten nonbelievers seven days a week for a mere $3 admission fee. Photos, newspaper clippings, grainy videos—even a plaster cast of a Skunk Ape's footprint—do their best to convince these "doubting Thomases." Says Shealy, "I don't have a choice to believe, because I've seen [the Skunk Ape] three times." We'll have to take his word for it.

# Weeki Wachee Springs

***Weeki Wachee, Florida***

Since 1947, Florida's Weeki Wachee Springs has enthralled people with its natural beauty, glass-bottom boat tours, and world-famous "mermaids."

In 1946, when former U.S. Navy man Newton Perry perfected hose breathing (the ability to breathe underwater via a compressor-fed air hose) at Weeki Wachee Springs, a door opened. Now it was suddenly possible to stage underwater shows in the 72-degree, crystal-clear spring. Perry set out to do just that.

By 1947, the first underwater theater was completed. This enabled tourists to view proceedings from below-ground rooms. It also ushered in the Weeki Wachee Mermaids.

There's something fabulously unreal about fish-tipped dancers performing an underwater ballet. From a campy act that includes more than a little humor to captivating choreographed moves that sometimes find the mermaids hanging motionless as if in space, the show has become a staple of Weeki Wachee. But it isn't the only thing out of the ordinary at the spring.

Glass-bottom boat tours pick up where the underwater show leaves off. As the small boats make their way through the 45-foot-deep spring (the spring links to a cave system that's been explored to 403 feet, making it the deepest naturally formed spring in the United States), manatees, fish, turtles—even the occasional alligator—come into view. Every so often, the mermaids are spotted doing their act, captivating the crowd as they hold their breath for more than two minutes.

## Carnival Museum

***Mobile, Alabama***

This museum, which traces the history of Carnival in Mobile, acts as a Mardi Gras primer. Who knew that Mardi Gras (French for *Fat Tuesday*, the final and most spectacular day of Carnival) was first celebrated in the United States more than 300 years ago? And how many realize that Mobile beat New Orleans to the punch as the birthplace of Mardi Gras in America?

Through displays, exhibits, artifacts, and art, the Mobile Carnival Museum educates as it entertains. Visitors will find elaborate gowns and trains worn by past Carnival queens alongside flamboyant outfits worn by Mardi Gras's many jesters. Posters, ball invitations, and interactive exhibits round out the celebratory repertoire.

## Unclaimed Baggage Center

***Scottsboro, Alabama***

At the Unclaimed Baggage Center (UBC), shoppers will find a wealth of bargains. Unfortunately, their gain is directly linked to someone else's loss. Horror stories concerning lost luggage are as common as flight delays these days. Many frequent flyers actually *expect* to lose a bag over the course of a year. When this unfortunate occurrence takes place, a portion of the bounty can end up here.

After a 90-day waiting period (just to make things right and proper) the free-for-all begins. UBC carries virtually everything that people drag onto airplanes, so its departments read much like Macy's. Looking for ladies and men's clothing? They're here. Digital cameras and electronics float your boat? Dig in. From fine jewelry to Persian rugs, artwork to luggage (surprise!), this place has you covered. Greatest find thus far? A 40.95-karat natural emerald.

Since the inventory is constantly revolving, treasure-hunting types consider the place more of a happening than a mere store. "Unclaimed Baggage Center gets nearly one million visitors annually, making it one of Alabama's top attractions," says the *London Free Press*. Sounds about right *and* wrong when you get right down to it.

**QUICK FACT**

Over the years, the Unclaimed Baggage Center has had some unusual finds. Like the rattlesnake employees found packed away in an unclaimed suitcase. Or the doll with $500 hidden inside. Sounds like every day is an adventure at this place!

## Spear Hunting Museum

***Summerdale, Alabama***

Eugene C. Morris desperately wants the world to know that he's a spear hunter. Plastered on the side of his museum is this boastful proclamation: "The Greatest Living Spear Hunter in the World." Since Morris claims to have taken more than 400 big-game animals with his trusty lance, we'll have to take his word for it.

Within his 7,600-square-foot display, Morris's fleshy spoils are displayed beside a vast assortment of spears. Realizing that many peaceful people take exception to his chosen sport, the hunter offers no apologies. "They are just plain, flat-out not rational or even sane," says the spear-chucker when he describes the "don't kill anything" crowd.

In the souvenir area, a four-bladed steel "killer" spear is offered for sale beside a host of other deadly implements. While we'll "spear" clear of the great hunting debate, we will say that the Spear Hunting Museum comes right to the point. Take that as you will.

## Ave Maria Grotto

***Cullman, Alabama***

This "Jerusalem in Miniature" is the lifework of Benedictine monk Joseph Zoettl (1878–1961). Using stone, concrete, and whatever building materials he could scrounge together, Brother Zoettl reproduced 125 of the world's most famous buildings and shrines in miniature and deposited them on a steep hillside.

Spread over a four-acre site, Zoettl's creations include the Vatican's St. Peter's Basilica, the Monte Casino Abbey, the Alamo, the Leaning Tower of Pisa, and the Hiroshima Peace Church.

Zoettl spent some 50 years building his miniature city—no small feat given the fact that the holy man was afflicted with a hunched back. Still, the talented monk persevered and was able to move mountains. Little ones, in this case, but mountains nonetheless.

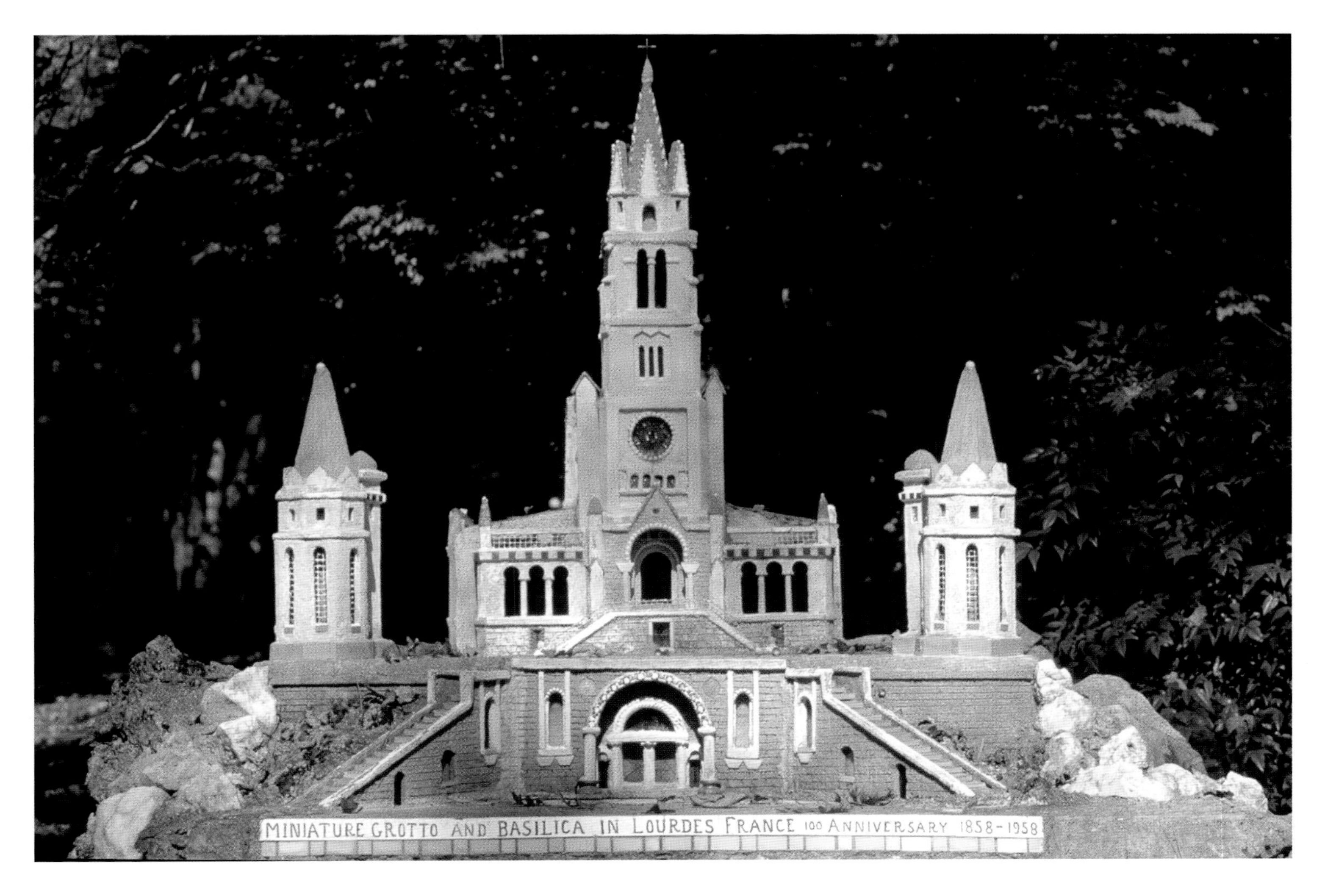

## World's Largest Chair

***Anniston, Alabama***

The battle for World's Largest Chair has been an unexpectedly heated one. This chair, located in Anniston, Alabama, was dubbed the World's Largest by *Guinness World Records* in 1982, but it has since been outseated by chairs in other cities. Nevertheless, we think it's worthy of amazing and unusual status. After all, it's bound to make a *big* impression on visitors.

QUICK FACT

There is no admission fee for the museum, but donations are accepted and appreciated.

## Jim Henson Museum

***Leland, Mississippi***

This small museum, located at Leland's Chamber of Commerce, celebrates Jim Henson (1936–1990), the creator of Kermit the Frog, Miss Piggy, and other beloved Muppet characters.

Henson grew up in Leland and incorporated snippets from his childhood into his richly humorous characters. Kermit, for instance, actually evolved from Kermit Scott, a childhood playmate.

Information and photos cataloguing Henson's life are found here, alongside Muppet dolls and memorabilia. A wooden cutout of Kermit, all "frogged-up" in his finest threads, stands sentry rain or shine in front of the museum. Its obvious message? It ain't easy being green!

## Graceland Too

***Holly Springs, Mississippi***

If thoughts of the "King" turn your knees to Jell-O, know that you are not alone. Superfan Paul McLeod has assembled a world-class shrine to Elvis that is only a few ticks behind the rock-and-roller's genuine Graceland digs.

Items housed within McLeod's antebellum mansion run the gamut from original carpet remnants (taken from Graceland) to thousands of Presley's 45-rpm records. There's a gold lamé jumpsuit that McLeod insists he'll be buried in, a petal from the first flower laid on Elvis's grave, newspaper articles, posters, magazine covers—virtually everything one might ever seek in Elvisdom, along with a whole bunch of things that they might not.

## Christ of the Ozarks

***Eureka Springs, Arkansas***

In yet another giant testament to faith, this 67-foot rendition of Christ stands tall atop Magnetic Mountain. Somewhat cartoonlike in appearance, the giant statue has earned such unflattering nicknames as "Gumby Jesus" and "Our Milk Carton with Arms."

Christ of the Ozarks was originally intended to be the centerpiece of a religious theme park, but that venture never came to pass. Today, the statuesque savior welcomes visitors to an outdoor passion play held at a nearby 4,100-seat amphitheater.

**QUICK FACT**

Christ of the Ozarks enjoyed a very brief moment in the spotlight in the 2005 film *Elizabethtown.*

## Crater of Diamonds State Park

***Murfreesboro, Arkansas***

Crater of Diamonds State Park is billed as the "world's only diamond site where you can search and keep what you find."

The 37-acre field, the eroded surface of an ancient, gem-bearing volcanic pipe, beckons get-rich-quick types with its implied promise. Several large diamonds found here have been cut into valuable "D" flawless stones. That said, the majority of stones uncovered by diamond prospectors are of the "rough" variety. Translation: They're worth a couple of bucks, tops, and are generally kept as souvenirs.

Still, the fun is in the hunt. And who knows? You may be the one to unearth the next "biggie."

**QUICK FACT**

The most recent "biggie" found at the park was discovered in 2006. The Roden Diamond, as it is called, was a whopping 6.35 karats. Happy hunting!

## Peavy's Monster Mart

***Fouke, Arkansas***

Fouke, Arkansas, is famous for the Boggy Creek Monster—a half-man, half-ape creature along the lines of Bigfoot. For visitors who yearn to know more, Peavy's Monster Mart is their number-one stop.

The monster was first sighted in these parts back in the 1940s. Eventually, he'd become so popular that a series of movies, beginning with *The Legend of Boggy Creek* (1972), would commit him to hairy folk history.

At Peavy's, a rather nondescript service station, the "Boggy Creek Monster" makes an appearance in the form of a wooden cutout board.

Those wishing to learn more about the monster amble inside. There they will behold a plaster cast of Bigfoot, Peavy's featured exhibit since the Boggy Creek Monster's cast was supposedly lost to fire. After the excitement dies down, they continue on their journey all the richer for their efforts.

## Abita Mystery House/ UCM Museum

***Abita Springs, Louisiana***

Billed as Louisiana's Most Eccentric Attraction, this wonderful mishmash contains just about everything a traveler on a strange and unusual trip looks for. Take the sign that says, "If you have 3 or more it's a collection—A musuem (sic) has over 3 collections." The obvious misspelling will annoy English teachers, but it spells f-u-n for us!

The "musuem" contains thousands of found objects and homemade inventions. Take a gander at the wind-driven whirligig standing beside a "Bassigator" (a 22-foot cross between a bass and an alligator). Next to these are a "Dogigator" (think alligator/dog crossbreed) and a Slipstream trailer that's been taken over by alien forces. How can we tell? A flying saucer has crashed into its side.

Owner John Preble used more than 50,000 recycled objects to create the bulk of his displays, and humor has been a steering force. At "Lil Dub's BBQ" diorama we're invited to "eat here and get gas." Another display puts an oil refinery smack up against an antebellum plantation. This is Louisiana, after all.

## Home of the World's Tabasco Sauce Supply

***Avery Island, Louisiana***

Who would guess that all of the world's Tabasco sauce hails from this one island? It's true. Despite the fact that Tabasco sauce labels are printed in 21 languages and dialects, the sauce itself comes from here. Even more impressive, the McIlhenny Company, which started producing the sauce in 1868, still oversees the operation.

For those who've never experienced the "burn" of Tabasco sauce, a quick primer: The original Tabasco sauce measured 2,500 to 5,000 Scoville heat units (SHU) on the Scoville Scale. Translation: It was one *hot* sauce. It is currently marketed in 160 different countries, and more than 700,000 bottles are produced each day at the Avery Island plant.

Tours of the facility are said to be one hot ticket. "See the original hottie" might make for a memorable slogan.

### Too Hot to Handle

The Scoville Scale was named for its creator, Wilbur Scoville. In 1912, this American chemist devised a test to rate the heat of chili peppers. The scale ranges from 0 to 16,000,000 SHU. The hottest pepper in the world ranks a whopping 1,001,304 SHU.

QUICK FACT

The house of voodoo currently standing at 1020 St. Ann Street in New Orleans was never actually occupied by Marie Laveau. This house marks the approximate site of the home that Laveau inhabited until her death. The original cottage was demolished in 1903.

## Marie Laveau's House of Voodoo

***New Orleans, Louisiana***

Why visit knock-off voodoo shops when you can see the real thing? Marie Laveau's House of Voodoo is said to exist on the actual spot that legendary Voodoo queen Marie Laveau II called home. In fact, the queen is said to haunt her old haunts.

The store, rather smallish for so weighty an enterprise, features a Voodoo museum and sells Voodoo paraphernalia to neophytes (a.k.a. tourists) as well as seasoned practitioners. As one of New Orleans's most popular attractions, it's just the place to score that hard-to-find Voodoo doll or gris-gris bag.

## Chapter Four

# THE MIDWEST

The Midwest, our nation's heartland, a bountiful land of milk, honey, and most every crop found on good mother Earth, may strike some as an unlikely place to encounter the amazing and unusual—but that may be just the reason it's so chock-full of oddities.

This natural canvas has spawned more than its share of whimsical wonders. From Carhenge in Alliance, Nebraska, to Leila's Hair Museum in Independence, Missouri, the region is rife with the delightful and offbeat.

But don't jump to conclusions. In addition to the frivolous and absurd, the Midwest lays claim to some genuine superlatives. Whether it's a jaw-dropper like the World's Largest Ball of Twine in Darwin, Minnesota, or an "ohmigosh!" producer like the Corn Palace in Mitchell, South Dakota, each unique item demonstrates the midwesterner's penchant for uniting the practical with the playful and proves that there's nothing flat in this region apart from the terrain.

*Carhenge, Alliance, Nebraska*

## Chateau Laroche

***Loveland, Ohio***

With Chateau Laroche, a full-scale medieval castle, Sir Harry Andrews (1890–1981) brought the middle ages to Loveland, Ohio.

According to published reports, pacifist Andrews served as a medic during World War I. After saving the life of a French earl's son, the soldier was knighted for his efforts. When he returned to the United States, Andrews settled in Cincinnati and formed a youth group called the "Knights of the Golden Trail." He vowed to build a castle for his knights in the making.

In 1929, Andrews purchased land beside the Little Miami River and started the project; he was still working on the castle at the time of his death in 1981. Construction efforts had included some 2,600 sacks of cement, 54,000 five-gallon buckets of dirt, and 56,000 pails of stone.

Today, the castle serves as the headquarters for the Knights of the Golden Trail. It is also open to less noble visitors, who are invited to tour the castle and learn all about Harry and his vision.

## Futuro

***Carlisle, Ohio***

The Futuro House of Carlisle, Ohio (one of a surprisingly large number of such structures located throughout the world), looks like it was lifted straight from a sci-fi flick. Is the house a classic case of humanistic life forms copying art? Perhaps. Is it off-the-charts bizarre? Without a doubt.

The concept of the Futuro house was originally designed by Finnish architect Matti Suuronen in 1965. The Futuro in Carlisle features two oblong silver saucers connected by a tubular walkway. Nicknamed the "mating flying-saucer house" for this distinctive feature, the "risqué" structure really does come across as two spaceships "cozying up" for a visit. The residence is currently inhabited (by humanoids, we assume).

**QUICK FACT**
The first Futuro house was built in Finland in 1968.

## "Y" Bridge

***Zanesville, Ohio***

One can only wonder how many unwitting souls have driven off the "Y" bridge in the city of Zanesville, Ohio. Of course, it's not a tough mistake to make on a bridge that's shaped like the letter "Y." Who's behind such a funky configuration, you might wonder?

In its first incarnation, as the Third Street Bridge (1813), designer Moses Dillon explained that the bridge would run "from the point opposite Main Street of Zanesville to an island at the mouth of the Licking [River], thence north and south each way across the mouth of Licking Creek."

Since then, the unique span at the convergence of the Muskingum and Licking rivers has been rebuilt four times; its latest upgrade took place in 1984. As one of only two such bridges in the United States (the other is located in Galena, Missouri), the structure has become the pride of Zanesville. Citizens say that after crossing the span, you can still be on the side of the river from which you originated. A bird's-eye view of the bridge shows that the boast is only partially true. No matter. It's still one crazy structure.

Today, the bridge stands gussied up with wider lanes and a modern stoplight at its critical "Y" intersection. These, we presume, will keep distracted drivers from becoming sudden swimmers.

**QUICK FACT**
The "Y" Bridge is on the National Register of Historic Places.

# World's Largest Cuckoo Clock

***Sugarcreek, Ohio***

In a region that's renowned for big quirky things, a huge cuckoo clock makes great sense. At least that's what Ohio clockmakers apparently thought when they undertook the building of the World's Largest Cuckoo Clock. While the "world's largest" claim is a bit uncertain these days (at present, the timepiece is caught up in a cuckoo battle with another giant in Frankenmuth, Michigan), the clock's largesse is certainly not.

Picture this: Every half hour, dwarf-size figures in the form of a Bavarian band move across the clock's stage. This sets a dancing couple into motion, the maiden doing pirouettes around a slower-moving man decked out in suspender shorts and lederhosen. Polka music plays throughout, and the band slowly retreats to their standby position—out of sight until the next half-hour is reached.

Constructed over a 12-year period from 1962 to 1974, the clock stands some 23½ feet tall, 24 feet long, and 13½ feet wide. In 2010, the clock was purchased at auction by Walnut Creek Cheese. It was subsequently moved to Sugarcreek, Ohio, known as the "Little Switzerland of Ohio."

## World's Largest Basket

***Newark, Ohio***

Employees at the Longaberger Company must feel a duality of purpose. Are associates headed for work each day, or are they headed off to a picnic? And when they do arrive at headquarters, are they expected to create or *recreate*? To a casual observer, both approaches seem to apply. How can this be? It's quite simple, really. The Longaberger Company makes handwoven baskets, and its headquarters in Newark, Ohio, is one BIG basket. A bit confused? No need. It all comes down to simple "basketology."

Dave Longaberger, the company's founder, is something of a visionary. While it can be argued that many such entrepreneurs fall into this category, Dave went his fellow "movers and shakers" one better when he built his headquarters in the shape of a picnic basket in 1997.

The basket is actually a faithful replica of Longaberger's "Medium Market Basket," but at 160 times its size; that's pretty much where any similarity ends. At 208 feet by 142 feet at its roofline, this is one HUGE basket. It's also one large office building—hence the confusion.

At night, the picnic basket is bathed in light—a situation that could potentially attract hungry marauders. But there's no need to worry. At this gargantuan size, this is one picnic basket even Yogi Bear couldn't steal!

**QUICK FACT**
The Longaberger Company began in 1973 with just five basket makers.

## Jungle Jim's International Market

***Fairfield, Ohio***

**QUICK FACT**
More than 50,000 shoppers patronize Jungle Jim's each week.

It was bound to happen. In a country that is enamored of theme parks, theme weddings, and theme dining, how far behind could a theme supermarket be?

Jungle Jim's is an operation aimed directly at "foodies." According to founder James O. Bonaminio, the market's first rule is to treat customers like gold, and its second rule is to have fun while doing so. Judging by their bizarre store displays, Jim and company are having an absolute ball.

When people say "it's a jungle out there," negativity prevails. When Jim's shoppers say "it's a jungle *in* there," they are speaking literally and quite lovingly. In addition to the expected food items, Jim's 300,000-square-foot building features fiberglass elephants, gorilla statues, super-tall giraffes—even a gushing waterfall.

There are also nonjungle bits and pieces thrown in just for fun. Good examples are the SS *Minnow*, a 40-foot-long shrimp boat featuring an animated band, and Soupy the Soup Can Man, a five-and-a-half-foot-tall, animatronic, singing soup can. Each aisle seems to lead to something wackier than the one before it. Our favorite untamed bit? Fully equipped restrooms disguised as Porta-Johns. Now *that's* pretty wild!

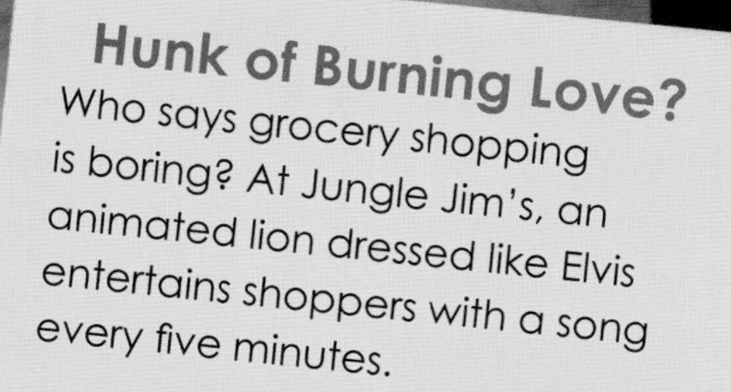

**Hunk of Burning Love?**
Who says grocery shopping is boring? At Jungle Jim's, an animated lion dressed like Elvis entertains shoppers with a song every five minutes.

*The Uniroyal Tire put the "wheel" in Ferris Wheel at the 1964–1965 World's Fair* (above).

## World's Largest Tire

***Allen Park, Michigan***

Originally built as the Uniroyal Ferris Wheel for the 1964–1965 World's Fair, this 12-ton, 80-foot-tall chunk of "rubber" has been on a roll over the years. After the fair concluded and its 24 gondolas were removed, the tire made its way to Allen Park to be outfitted for its new mission. It would still hawk Uniroyal Tires, but it would now stand motionless.

Over the years, the outsize hoop has evolved from a bias-ply whitewall to an all-season radial, and changes continue to be made. One change not planned for the tire is its ownership. Uni, Roy, and Al simply don't roll that way.

**QUICK FACT**

In 1998, Uniroyal pierced the tread of the tire with an 11-foot-long nail to show off their puncture-resistant Tiger Paw Nailgard tire. Luckily, surgery removed the 250-pound protrusion in 2003, and the tire rolled on.

## American Museum of Magic

***Marshall, Michigan***

When modern-day magicians David Blaine and Criss Angel attempt a trick, they often expand on ideas originally dreamt up by the old masters. Harry Houdini, The Great Blackstone, and a score of others helped pave the way for today's breed; in turn, these newcomers give back by paying allegiance to their mystical predecessors. With such exchanges in mind, wouldn't it be great if there were a grand repository where magicians and fans alike could draw inspiration? There is. The American Museum of Magic lies a bit off the spotlight circuit in Marshall, Michigan, but it captivates nonetheless.

Bob Lund began collecting magicians' artifacts in the mid-1930s and didn't stop until his death in 1995. His cache is considered to be the world's largest privately owned collection of magic bits. Showcased in a three-story building, Lund's museum catalogs magic's numinous path from the days of Jean Eugene Robert-Houdin (Houdini's namesake) clear through to today's headliners.

Within the museum's walls, "magicphiles" will find props, posters, costumes, films—virtually everything pertaining to magic. Lund even acquired the original Houdini "Milk Can" and Harry Blackstone's "Levitating Skull." It's unclear whether Houdini makes ethereal appearances on Halloween, but if the Great One were to return, we're certain he'd drop in for a visit.

# World's Longest Front Porch

***Grand Hotel, Mackinac Island, Michigan***

With a commanding view of Lake Huron, it's not surprising that the historic Grand Hotel features a magnificent front porch. Since the establishment overlooks a waterway connected by the Mackinac Bridge (once considered the world's longest suspension bridge between anchorages), it's only fitting that this porch is equally world-trouncing.

The opulent summer hotel was built in 1887 by a company that owned railroads and steamships. It was aimed at affluent vacationers who would use these conveyances to reach the island—a veritable win/win proposition for the joint concern. To distinguish the Grand Hotel from other inns of its day, builders installed a long front porch. And we do mean l-o-n-g.

At the length of two football fields, plus 60 additional feet for good measure, the 660-foot porch is the longest in the world. People come from far and wide to walk its decking and to take in its outstanding views.

**QUICK FACT**

The Grand Hotel has been patronized by five U.S. presidents (Harry Truman, John Kennedy, Gerald Ford, George H. W. Bush, and Bill Clinton). Perhaps the bigwigs were scoping out retirement locations?

## Marvelous Marvin's Mechanical Museum

***Farmington Hills, Michigan***

Since 1990, when Marvin Yagoda turned his obsession for arcades and sideshows into a museum, we have all benefited. Who could live without old-time coin-operated machines or robotic fortune tellers? And that's just the normal stuff. Yagoda's museum also features the Cardiff Giant, a knockoff of the "real" fake figure now located in Cooperstown, New York, and "The Drunkard's Dream," a 1935 coin-operated machine that illustrates what one sees when they've gone beyond their limit. The museum is so very offbeat it's listed in the *World Almanac*'s "100 Most Unusual Museums in the United States."

Approximately 5,500 feet of floor space play host to curiosities, animatronic dummies, pinball machines, posters, love and torture machines, and all manner of other techno-goodies. "Love and torture [machines] are the favorites," declares Yagoda. Somehow, we believe him.

After noticing that the Cardiff Giant was pulling in huge audiences, P. T. Barnum tried to rent him for display. He was unsuccessful. The showman then made a duplicate copy of the giant and started selling tickets. The newly made, "fake" version did so well it actually outsold the original fake stone man in Cooperstown. How's that for knowing your audience? The outsize duplicate figure currently resides at Marvelous Marvin's.

**QUICK FACT**
Admission to Marvin's is free.

## RV Hall of Fame

***Elkhart, Indiana***

The Recreational Vehicle (RV) Hall of Fame is a celebration of road trip adventure. Built in 1991, this 100,000-square-foot facility features Winnebagos, Airstreams, Holiday Ramblers, and scores of lesser-known vehicles. The hall-of-fame section includes the names of industry bigwigs and innovators. Dedicated RVers should be excused for not knowing any of them—after all, they were too busy RVing to pay proper attention! They'd have it no other way.

## 1950s Hobby Shop Replica

***National Model Aviation Museum***
***Muncie, Indiana***

When you step through the door of the 1950s Hobby Shop Replica, you may as well be flashing back in time. So faithful is the reproduction, one can almost smell the pungent yet intoxicating scent of cement struggling to unite confusing parts in a Control Line model kit.

Even the shop's outer facade triggers memories and will prompt those of a certain age to recall happy jaunts to their local hobby store. To complete the illusion, a friendly looking storekeeper named "Mel" stands at the ready to answer probing questions and tally up one's goodies. Ah, yes. Was life ever sweeter than this?

## Giant Ice Cream Man

***Montpelier, Indiana***

Looming over an ice cream stand and gift shop, a man of uncommon size—about 25 feet tall—clutches a cone. This giant, replete with red blazer, wears a look of supreme satisfaction on his kisser. And why shouldn't he? With the Tin Lizzy Ice Cream Shop churning out endless refills below, he may well be in ice cream heaven. Yum!

## Hippie Memorial

***Arcola, Illinois***

"What a long strange trip it's been." So said the Grateful Dead in their popular song, "Truckin." But the verse could just as easily apply to the life of Bob Moomaw, creator of the "World's Only Hippie Memorial."

At some 62 feet long, Moomaw's personal journey (he lived for exactly 62 years) is cataloged in segments. The Great Depression, World War II, and 1950s hypocrisy crowds the first third. Next up are the Kennedy era and Moomaw's beloved Hippie invasion—a time span expressed by colorful peace symbols, freedom of expression scribbling, and a license plate reading "WOODSTC." This era takes the memorial clear through to 1980, the year that Ronald Reagan was elected president. Moomaw celebrates this "downer" with 18 feet of plain rusted scrap.

Bob Moomaw disagreed with a great many things and an equal number of people during his lifetime, but he believed strongly in freedom of expression and the right to dissent. By all accounts, he'd fight to the death to preserve either. His Hippie Memorial stands as a fitting tribute to a man who was a thorn in the side of "established" America. We think that's groovy.

## Ed Debevic's

***Chicago, Illinois***

Can you imagine a bistro where the hired help treat their customers like swill? And if that's not wacky enough, can you fathom loyal patrons who will return again and again for such abuse? Well, imagine no more. Ed Debevic's Restaurant prides itself on such mistreatment, and their customers can't seem to get enough.

The first tip that something is different comes in the waitstaff's garb. Silly and outlandish doesn't begin to explain the ridiculous getups found at Ed's place. When waiters take orders, they'll make fun of the slowest-ordering person at the table and issue sarcastic wisecracks throughout the process. If anyone dares to order a beverage refill, they'll tersely be told "get your own!"

Perhaps the wisenheimer approach began with Debevic himself. Taught the restaurant trade by a no-nonsense woman named "Lill" (of Lill's Homesick Diner in Talooca, Illinois), Ed admired her "eat and get out" policy so very much, he later applied it to his own business. Says Debevic, "If you like what you're eatin', order more. If you don't, there's the door!" In our amazing and unusual world, this sounds like a solid business model.

## Henry's Rabbit Ranch

***Staunton, Illinois***

Rich and Linda Henry opened their attraction more than a decade ago after noticing a lack of visitor centers and souvenir stands along Route 66 (a.k.a. the Mother Road).

Henry's features a vintage gas station that blurs the line between modernity and Route 66's heyday. In truth, it has never been a filling station but is just a faithfully executed mockup.

Then there are the rabbits. The explosion began soon after the couple's daughter obtained a pair. When their offspring reached critical mass, father Rich intervened and opened the rabbit ranch.

Each day, the couple tends to their rabbits and does their level best to answer tourists' questions. Since both grew up in the shadow of the famous route, they're more than up to the task.

## World's Largest Catsup Bottle

***Collinsville, Illinois***

Water towers come in all different shapes and sizes these days, but it's likely you've never seen one that looks like it would be good with a hot dog!

Built almost 60 years ago, the Brooks Old Original Tangy Catsup bottle is based on a real catsup product that can still be purchased today. The original company, which was called the Triumph Catsup and Pickle Company, was owned by brothers Everett and Elgin Brooks but passed hands (and changed names) several times before the popular catsup was born. Not only did the company survive the Great Depression, but it also thrived through the 1940s.

Plans for the 100,000-gallon water tower were drawn up in 1947 as an amusing form of advertisement. Two years later, the World's Largest Catsup Bottle stood 100 feet in the air. The bottle still stands today in its all-American red, white, and blue finery, thanks to a restoration project completed in 1995.

But does the bottle hold water or catsup? Ask the people of Collinsville and they will say, "We'll never tell."

**QUICK FACT**

Planning to visit the bottle? Aim to go during the World's Largest Catsup Bottle Festival held every summer for fun, food, and drink (and, of course, catsup tasting).

QUICK FACT

The Tower of Pisa is the crowning glory of the Leaning Tower YMCA, the facilities for which are located behind the famous replica.

## Tower of Pisa replica

***Niles, Illinois***

In 1934, local businessman Robert Ilg built a recreation park for his employees that consisted of two swimming pools, two cabanas, and one very unusual covering for the pools' water tank: a half-size replica of the Leaning Tower of Pisa. The existence of the tower made a bit more sense when Niles and Pisa consummated a sister-city relationship in 1991.

## Superman

***Metropolis, Illinois***

Metropolis, Illinois, with a population of 15,000 (including the city and the county), is not quite the Metropolis of DC Comics fame. But it predates Superman by a long shot, as it was founded in 1839. In 1972, the town decided to capitalize on the association and adopted the "Hometown of Superman" moniker. A seven-foot statue went up in 1986, only to be replaced seven years later by this more impressive 15-foot bronze.

**QUICK FACT**

In 2008, the town of Metropolis attempted to set a world record by gathering 122 men and women dressed as Superman around the Superman statue. The record they were after was "The Largest Gathering of People Dressed as Superman." The town is waiting for Guinness to verify their record.

## Giant Woman Statue

***Peoria, Illinois***

When a person drives past Peoria Plaza Tire, they might be excused for thinking that they're witnessing the "Attack of the 50-Foot Woman." In reality, this giant damsel is "only" 17.5 feet tall. Still, big is big.

In town since 1968, the ageless "Vanna Whitewall" (previously "Miss Uniroyal") isn't a jealous monster at all. She lives only to sell tires and hawk car repairs. At various times, the big gal has worn bikinis and skirts, and her hair color has seen some changes as well.

Her 108–72–108 measurements and 450-pound heft may not earn her a slot in a beauty contest, but she apparently plays well in Peoria.

**QUICK FACT**

Like many giant fiberglass women across America, Vanna Whitewall started life as a Miss Uniroyal in the 1960s. Her raised left hand was originally intended to display a Uniroyal tire for marketing purposes.

# Dr. Evermor's Forevertron

***North Freedom, Wisconsin***

Head south on highway 12 out of Baraboo, Wisconsin, and you could almost miss it—the World's Largest Scrap Metal Sculpture.

Sounds like a lofty designation for so obscure an object, but the title rings true. Situated across from the old Badger Army Ammunition Plant and nestled behind Delaney's Surplus, Dr. Evermor's Forevertron is marked by little signage and does not boast from the roadside. One must look closely for this structural wonder—or risk passing it by, forever.

A dirt road leads to the scrap metal behemoth, and it doesn't take long for visitors to appreciate the glory of Dr. Evermor's bizarre masterpiece. The 50-foot-high, 300-ton metal creation erupts from a clearing, brandishing ray guns, telescopes, and peculiar mechanical creatures. Looming iron insects, whimsical brass birds, and enormous alien contraptions add to an atmosphere that is weirdly carnival, and the air is almost electrically charged with the feeling that the thing could move at any second.

Capped by a copper-sheathed glass ball in the shape of an egg, this space-age creation is in fact anchored largely by old 19th-century industrial scrap: generators, thrusters, and carburetors from the age of steam power. Nods to an era long past are given by turn-of-the-century harvesters and aging wooden phone booths scattered about the place.

Dr. Evermor himself (or Tom Every, as the creator was known in his previous life as an industrial wrecker) would argue that the Forevertron isn't art for art's sake, exactly. Since 1983, he's been trying to put the "scrap" that he used to move to good use. And what a good use it is!

Oh, and there's one other thing. According to Dr. Evermor, "the Forevertron's purpose is to perpetuate [him] into heaven in a glass ball inside a copper egg on a magnetic lightning force beam." If you want to find out what that's all about, you'll have to pay him a visit.

### QUICK FACT

The Forevertron is constructed from many important historical objects, including an original decontamination chamber from one of the Apollo space missions.

## House on the Rock

***Spring Green, Wisconsin***

Capping a 60-foot geological formation named Deer Shelter Rock is one of the best-known architectural oddities in the United States. The House on the Rock (a parody of Frank Lloyd Wright's work) is the creation of Alex Jordan, who started building it in the 1940s as a vacation home near Spring Green, Wisconsin. He just kept on building, furnishing it with Asian art, a three-story bookcase, and anything else that captured his fevered imagination. He soon realized the place could lure tourists by the carload and started charging fifty cents for tours. Jordan sold the house in the late 1980s, but the place just keeps getting bigger and stranger by the year. With 14 unique and lavishly decorated rooms—including the Infinity Room, with 3,264 windows—and a surrounding complex that houses a miniature circus, the world's largest indoor carousel, and a full-fledged destination resort, the House on the Rock is at once wacky, tacky, innovative, and elegant.

## Statue of "Romeo," the Killer Elephant

***Delavan, Wisconsin***

In the 1800s, when 25 circuses wintered here, the town of Delavan was considered the "Circus Capital of the World." Needless to say, this place saw more than its share of pachyderms. Most of these behemoths did typical elephant tricks and acted in a typical elephant way. Then there was Romeo. Over a 15-year period, the "killer" elephant erased the lives of five trainers via foot stomps, crushing accidents, and tusk impalements. Why wasn't the animal executed for his crimes? Here's where it gets good.

They say Romeo suffered a broken heart when his beloved Juliet passed on to that great elephant graveyard in the sky. So, in effect, his attacks were really a form of grief resolution. It's a great story but not at all true. In reality, Romeo was one ornery elephant. Period.

For reasons perhaps unfathomable, the good people of Delavan decided to honor Romeo with a full-size statue. Their fiberglass re-creation features the bloodthirsty fellow standing on his hind legs, eager to trounce. Below him, a clown stands smiling, blissfully unaware of his impending doom. Folks, you just can't make this stuff up!

## Fred Smith's Wisconsin Concrete Park

***Phillips, Wisconsin***

Born in 1886, Fred Smith operated as a north woods lumberjack until 1949. During his retirement—a time when many others relax and celebrate past victories—Smith got busy. *Real* busy.

The self-taught sculptor would build a veritable city of wood-framed concrete figures and distribute them around his Rock Garden Tavern, a business he acquired while lumberjacking. In the end, Smith's park included miners, cowboys, Indians, and soldiers—all congregated in a splendid mishmash of folksy art.

**QUICK FACT**

Just after Smith died in 1976, a storm leveled three-quarters of his figures. Luckily, the Kohler Foundation stepped in and restored all to their former glory.

## Paul and Matilda Wegner Grotto

### *Cataract, Wisconsin*

Borrowing a page from Fred Smith's playbook, Paul Wegner got antsy when confronted with retirement. In 1929, after visiting Holy Ghost Park in Dickeyville, Wisconsin, Wegner's eureka moment arrived. With help from wife Matilda, he would build a grotto from "found materials."

Actually, *grotto* is a somewhat misleading term in this case. The Wegners' series of concrete-and-glass sculptures are non-denominational and include such items as the *Bremen*, a 12-foot concrete model of the celebrated ocean liner; a glass church; an American flag; a peace model; and—to celebrate their 50th wedding anniversary—an ornate wedding cake.

After Paul's death in 1937, Matilda continued work on the grotto until she made her final exit in 1942. In 1986, the Kohler Foundation restored the grotto to its former glory and presented it as a gift to the county of Monroe.

(From left to right) *The sculptures at the grotto include a church, a wedding cake, and a replica of the* Bremen.

## Shrine to Anglers

***Hayward, Wisconsin***

The centerpiece of the National Fresh Water Fishing Hall of Fame, these fish are so big there's no need for exaggeration. From tip to tail, the concrete, steel, and fiberglass muskie *(right)* is 140 feet in length and 4½ stories tall. There's a museum in its belly, and its toothy maw doubles as an observation platform. Adjacent to this really big fish is a four-building museum complex. Talk about an angler's dream comes true! The museum features such treasures as 300 mounted trophy fish, fishing artifacts, and a variety of rods and reels. Don't let this attraction be the one that got away!

## World's Largest Penny

***Woodruff, Wisconsin***

Here's a real heartwarmer. In 1953, Woodruff, Wisconsin, needed a new hospital. Doctor Kate Pelham Newcomb stepped in and lead the fund-raising charge by asking children to donate their pennies to the effort. The media seized upon the story, 1.7 million "Lincolns" came jingling in, and the hospital was built.

The World's Largest Penny commemorates the effort. So, how big is it? We'd put it at roughly ten feet in diameter. But size isn't everything. To Doctor Newcomb and a mass of generous children, it's undoubtedly the thought that counts.

**QUICK FACT**

The year 1953 is etched onto the one-inch-thick penny.

**QUICK FACT**

Each year, "Twine Ball Days" pay homage to the man who made it all possible.

## World's Largest Ball of Twine

***Darwin, Minnesota***

For the record, this is the "World's Largest Ball of Twine Rolled by One Man." His name was Francis A. Johnson. For 39 years, beginning in 1950, the committed (referring to his intentions, *not* his living arrangements) man labored for four hours each day to roll his dream. A crane assisted him when the giant ball grew too large. The ball eventually reached 12 feet in diameter and tipped the scales at a whopping 17,400 pounds.

When Francis passed away in 1989, the city of Darwin built a gazebo to properly house the record-breaking ball.

## SPAM Museum

***Austin, Minnesota***

When World War II soldiers saw a tin of SPAM coming their way, some reportedly said, "Ham, SPAM... Not that again!" Fortunately for Hormel Foods, maker of the famous luncheon meat, this was *not* the majority opinion.

In fact, SPAM (the lunch meat, not the unsolicited e-mail) is beloved. So much so that the company founded a mall-based museum in its honor in 1991. They chose Austin since it was here that George A. Hormel started his meat-processing dynasty way back in 1891. Since that time, the processed meat marvel has "spammed" the decades. As has the museum, which now finds itself in a larger, tastier facility.

Inside, an electronic counter tallies all SPAM production; 3,390 SPAM cans rise tall in the lobby; and a display shows how SPAM helped the Allies win World War II, keeping the world safe for democracy and future SPAM consumption. Spamalicious!

# Frank Lloyd Wright Gas Station

***Cloquet, Minnesota***

With modern-day gas stations taking us all "to the cleaners," a look at past offerings might be in order. In the case of Frank Lloyd Wright's contribution, that look is quite fetching indeed.

Celebrated architect Wright built his prototype service station under a distinctive copper roof in 1956. He assumed it would wow the nation. It didn't. In fact, most people passing through are oblivious to the great work standing over the requisite grease pit and gasoline drips, and that's a darned shame.

What folks might not realize is that this gas station is Wright's only realized design for "Broadacre City," his vision of a Utopian enclave. For this reason, a sign looms just below the giant Phillips 66 symbol. It reads: "World's only Frank Lloyd Wright service station." Despite an errant grease drop or three, it is that and so very much more.

## World's Largest Otter

***Fergus Falls, Minnesota***

As the seat of Otter Tail County, Fergus Falls is the fitting home of this 40-foot river otter. Made of concrete and metal, the oversize otter is biding its time near the waters of Grotto Lake in Adams Park. Nicknamed "Otto," the statue is the product of a high school project that celebrated Fergus Falls's centennial.

> **QUICK FACT**
> Stairs at the back of the statue enable visitors to pose for a photo with the jolly giant.

## Jolly Green Giant

***Blue Earth, Minnesota***

Ho, ho, ho—Green Giant! Wearing a size 78 shoe, this 55-foot-tall likeness pays homage to the third-most recognizable advertising icon of the 20th century. The statue's geographical significance: The Green Giant company began in the fertile farmland that surrounds Blue Earth. The town erected the statue in 1979 at a cost of $43,000.

## Saint Urho

***Menahga, Minnesota***

The patron saint of Finland, Urho cemented his case for sainthood when he drove grasshoppers from a vineyard in Finland. His accomplishments are celebrated at winter carnivals on both sides of the Atlantic, but Menahga's fete is the biggest and best. Today, Menahga's Saint Urho statue (complete with a giant grasshopper impaled on a pitchfork) is in heavy competition with a more abstract Urho carving across the state in Finland, Minnesota.

**QUICK FACT**

Saint Urho Day is celebrated on March 16.

## World's Largest Loon

***Virginia, Minnesota***

Tethered in the middle of Silver Lake in Virginia, Minnesota, by an unseen underwater chain, this 21-foot-long loon has been dubbed by locals as the world's largest floating loon.

QUICK FACT

The loon is Minnesota's state bird.

# Iron Man

***Chisholm, Minnesota***

Said to be the third-largest freestanding sculpture in the United States—outdone only by the Statue of Liberty and the St. Louis Arch—the 81-foot-tall statue (situated on a 150-ton red steel base) reminds visitors of the origins of the country's iron during much of the 20th century. Made of iron and steel and clad in bronze, copper, and brass sheathing, the Iron Man stands across from the Ironworld Discovery Center at the western entrance to Chisholm.

**QUICK FACT**

The Ironworld Discovery Center bills itself as "the largest museum complex in the region." Exhibits explore Minnesota's involvement in the iron mining industry. An open-pit mine is just a trolley ride away. Tours of the mine are available during the summer.

## World's Largest Bull

***Audubon, Iowa***

Named after local banker Albert Kruse, Albert the Bull is 45 tons of concrete Hereford. He was built as a monument to Operation T-Bone Days, an event held annually in September when local cattle board the train to the Chicago stockyards. At 30 feet tall and 33 feet long, Albert is a whole lot of bull.

**QUICK FACT**

The bull's internal steel frame is made of dismantled Iowa windmills.

## Grotto of Redemption

***West Bend, Iowa***

Had it not been for a bout of pneumonia, the Grotto of Redemption would never have been built. At least that's how legend explains it. Father Paul Matthias Dobberstein (1872–1954), a German immigrant, was said to have developed pneumonia while studying at the Seminary of St. Francis outside of Milwaukee. At death's door, the seminarian prayed to the Blessed Virgin Mary and vowed to build her a shrine if he was spared. The grotto stands as his fulfillment of that promise.

Starting in 1912 and ending upon his death, Dobberstein created nine distinct grottos, each depicting a scene from the life of Jesus Christ. Featuring the Ten Commandments, The Trinity Grotto, Stations of the Cross, Grotto of the Resurrection, the Stable of Bethlehem, and many more epic moments in the history of Christianity, the grotto is so immense, it is touted as the world's largest. While we can't speak to that, we can say that the grotto is profoundly beautiful. It's truly a gift to behold.

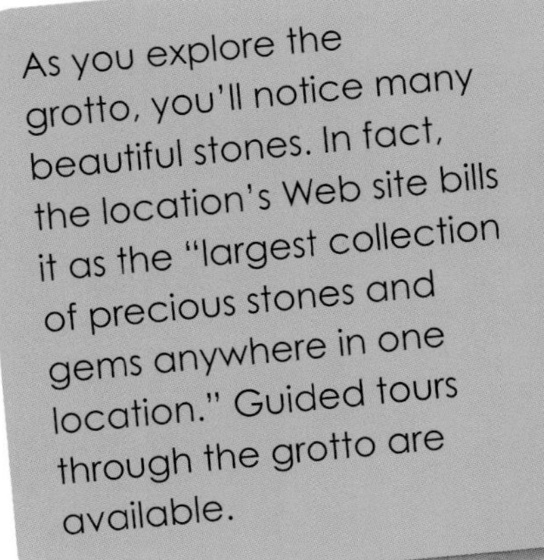

As you explore the grotto, you'll notice many beautiful stones. In fact, the location's Web site bills it as the "largest collection of precious stones and gems anywhere in one location." Guided tours through the grotto are available.

## Snake Alley

***Burlington, Iowa***

"There was a crooked man and he walked a crooked mile. . . ." Should this nursery rhyme spring to life, the crooked man might just go in search of Snake Alley for a sliver of his convoluted jaunt. Billed as the "Crookedest Street in the World" by none other than *Ripley's Believe It or Not*, Snake Alley would certainly be up any crooked man's (or woman's) alley!

Built in 1894 as a way to tame a steep hillside, the experimental design provided a direct link between Burlington's business district and a neighboring shopping area. Heralded as a "triumph in practical engineering" by local newspapers, the city proposed other such crooked streets, but the switchback design proved troublesome to horses, and plans were eventually scrapped.

The street remains intact to this day. Surprisingly, its brickwork is the very same batch originally laid down in 1894. How's that for far-sighted engineering?

## Field of Dreams

***Dyersville, Iowa***

"If you build it, he will come." This simple sentence from the 1989 movie *Field of Dreams* has joined a prestigious list of Hollywood's most memorable lines. The wildly successful film, rooted in baseball and the culmination of dreams, touched a certain chord in people. Stories about second chances have an uncanny way of doing that.

The field, with its outermost reaches dissolving mysteriously into rows of corn, was in fact very real. It was built at the Lansing farm in the summer of 1988 specifically for the movie.

When the film crew packed up, something rather startling happened. People, captivated by the story, flocked to see the field for themselves. They came from virtually everywhere and continue to come to this very day.

With a runaway hit movie driving interest in their ball field, owners of the *Field of Dreams* movie site probably could have charged admission. Much to their credit, they did not. Instead, they chose to maintain the field in a noncommercial fashion, a precept that mirrors the movie's theme. All visitors are invited to bring bats, balls, and gloves and "go the distance."

## Ida Grove Castles

***Ida Grove, Iowa***

Smack dab in the middle of America's heartland, a profusion of castles sure does stand out. Are they a promotion of some sort, designed for their incongruity? Not at all. They are simply the end result of one man's burning passion. And this man had the means to turn his obsession into reality.

He went by the noble tag Byron LeRoy Godberson (1925–2003). As a wealthy inventor and industrialist, Godberson could pretty much do as he pleased. If it was castles that he liked, then it was castles that he'd build. And build he did.

The town of Ida Grove looks like something straight out of the Middle Ages, with a castle tower welcoming visitors into town. Once inside, it becomes apparent that the castle theme is pervasive. The shopping center is shaped like a castle. So is the newspaper office. The local roller rink looks like something straight out of Disney World's Magic Kingdom. Even the town golf course features a medieval suspension bridge with imposing turrets on either end.

In addition to Ida Grove's castles, Godberson also created a half-scale replica of the sailing ship

*As you might imagine, Ida Grove attracts some attention. Here, a commercial is shot at Lake LaJune Estates.*

*This castle welcomes visitors to Ida Grove.*

the HMS *Bounty*. The grand ship took only 12 weeks to complete but when launched in Lake LaJune in 1970, it floated like a champ. As a Christmas gift to Godberson, a group of his employees summoned Captain Irving Johnson to Ida Grove in 1971. The seaman presented Godberson with a bronze fitting from the original *Bounty*. The replica still floats in the lake nearly four decades after its launch, a testament to its superb craftsmanship.

Godberson departed our mortal world in 2003. Was he summoned to the round table?

*The castle motif extends to the town's shopping center.*

**QUICK FACT**
Lake LaJune was named for Godberson's wife, LaJune.

*A replica of the HMS* Bounty *still floats in Lake LaJune.*

## Glore Psychiatric Museum
***St. Joseph, Missouri***

*The "Giant Patient Treadmill"*

*The "Tranquilizer Chair"*

In a country raving-mad for its "mad" movie heroes (think R. P. McMurphy from *One Flew over the Cuckoo's Nest* or Michael Myers from *Halloween*), the Glore Psychiatric Museum was probably inevitable.

Chronicling the 130-year history of Missouri's "State Lunatic Asylum No. 2," the museum features replicas, artifacts, visual aids, and interactive displays that recall a time in psychiatric history when words for mental illness were more pointed and public perceptions were more narrow.

Founder George Glore (an employee of Missouri's mental health system) spent 41 years assembling this collection into one so vast, it's recognized as "one of the 50 most unusual museums in the country."

Strange exhibits abound, but a few standouts are the "Bath of Surprise," a contraption that dumped a patient into icy water, and the "Giant Patient Treadmill," a "gerbilesque" megawheel where patients could walk their troubles away. One look at the treacherous "Tranquilizer Chair," and a patient could almost be scared out of insanity. Almost.

## Leila's Hair Museum

***Independence, Missouri***

While Leila's Hair Museum sounds like it might feature luxurious tresses and locks, it actually displays items that were *made* from hair. Okay, so it's still plenty weird.

Cosmetologist Leila Cohoon was in a pickle in 1990. Her burgeoning hair-wreath collection was forcing her out of her digs. Confronted with the reality of losing her hairy companions forever, Cohoon chose to allot them a display space at her new cosmetology studio.

Since then, the follicles have thrived. On display are some 2,000 pieces of hair jewelry, 150 hair wreaths, and a vast assortment of other hair-related items. "It could possibly be the only hair museum in the United States, maybe the world," boasts Leila. We shudder to think that this is true. There should be more. Hairs to us all!

## Dalton Defenders Museum

***Coffeyville, Kansas***

By the late 1800s, citizens of the West were quickly losing their patience with lawlessness and the perpetrators that forced it upon them. So on October 5, 1892, when the legendary Dalton Gang rode into Coffeyville hoping to separate the town's banks from their money, the citizens decided to take a stand.

When the Daltons tried to launch their escape after the robbery, citizens armed to the teeth opened fire. The gun battle would leave four of the five gang members dead and would claim the lives of four Coffeyville defenders.

The Dalton Defenders Museum pays homage to its martyred liberators with a collection of photos and artifacts and has even seen fit to preserve the actual vault doorway of the banks. Perhaps their most prized possession is a wall-size photo of the four Dalton boys lying lifeless on a board. " 'Twas the defenders that brought them down," the curator will quickly remind you. Indeed it was.

ON OCTOBER 5, 1892 THE DALTON GANG RODE INTO
COFFEYVILLE, KANSAS, TO ROB THE CONDON AND FIRST
NATIONAL BANKS. FOLLWING A 12-MINUTE GUN BATTLE, FOUR
MEMBERS OF THE DALTON GANG WERE KILLED-BOB & GRAT DALTON
BILL POWER AND DICK BROADWELL. EMMET DALTON SURVIVED.
FOUR COURAGEOUS CITIZENS ALSO LAY DEAD-GEORGE CUBINE,
CHARLES CONNELLY, CHARLES BROWN AND LUCIUS BALDWIN.

# Don Kracht's Castle Island

***Junction City, Kansas***

Who says math teachers lack imagination? As the builder of his very own medieval fortress, retired teacher Don Kracht dispels this silly notion quicker than a charging knight thrusts his lance.

And while we're slaying stereotypes, here's another one. Don Kracht never harbored visions of building a castle. "The castle just kinda came to me," says the unassuming man, who went in search of projects for his retirement. "I just started doing it."

He most certainly did. Kracht's castle features bridges, sculptures, balconies, turrets, a courtyard fountain, gargoyles and angels, spiral staircases, and of course, the requisite lookout tower.

Kracht continually adds items to his castle; as a result, its features keep multiplying. We'd expect no less from an "unimaginative" math teacher.

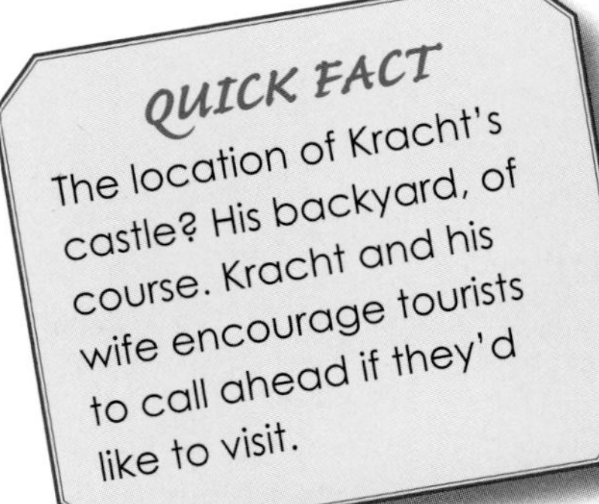

## World's Largest Atomic Cannon

### *Junction City, Kansas*

There are booms, and there are *booms*. The destructive force produced by America's atomic cannons of the 1950s clearly fell into the latter category.

Designed to lob nuclear shells at enemy forces while maintaining a safe distance, atomic cannons could reportedly hurl a 280mm shell up to 20 miles. This buffer zone was necessary since the bomb's yield was in the range of 15 kilotons, or 15,000 tons of TNT, precisely the figure associated with the historic blast at Hiroshima.

A handful of these misery-makers exist, but the unit at Junction City is purportedly the world's largest. Although deactivated in 1963, the launcher shows how very serious America's Cold War fears were. The fact that the cannon is now displayed in a public park does little to soften its original intent.

## Monkey Island

### *Independence, Kansas*

"Miss Able," a rhesus monkey hailing from Ralph Mitchell Zoo's Monkey Island, became one of the first living beings (alongside "Miss Baker," a squirrel monkey) to survive a trip into space aboard *Jupiter AM-18* on May 28, 1959.

The pint-size primate withstood speeds in excess of 10,000 miles per hour during her heroic journey. Sadly, she died a day later during surgery to remove an electrode.

Originally built in 1932, Miss Able's former home still operates, but it's a bit grown over these days. A prominent sign pays homage to the hairy dynamo that never had a chance to enjoy her fame.

# Big Brutus

***West Mineral, Kansas***

Big Brutus, a genuine "monster" truck, looms large at West Mineral's Mined Land Wildlife Area.

Calling Big Brutus large is like calling Einstein smart. At 16 stories tall (160 feet) and 11 million pounds, this electric earth-moving shovel seems as if it could push the earth off its axis.

Designed to mine coal from southeastern Kansas coal beds, Brutus was active from 1962 to 1974. The behemoth's great hunger for electricity proved its ultimate downfall. Big Brutus wasn't the first to be done in by gluttony, and he certainly won't be the last. Rest in peace, big boy.

**QUICK FACT**
Brutus's shovel was so large that when full, its contents could fill three railroad cars.

## Concrete Teepee

***Lawrence, Kansas***

When this giant teepee found its way onto the scene around 1930, the Wild West era had long passed. People now needed a place to sleep as they "rode" their gas-guzzling "horses" across the range, and the "Indian Village" complex was happy to oblige with a restaurant, filling station, and motor court dotted with smaller teepees.

Travelers could step into an enormous weatherproof teepee at the center of the complex to conduct their business. At 33 feet in diameter, more than a few "greenhorns" could be accommodated. Today, all that remains of the operation are a few abandoned outbuildings and the big teepee itself—slowly decaying mementos of a simpler, more playful time.

## Dorothy's House

***Liberal, Kansas***

"There's no place like home," chanted *The Wizard of Oz*'s Dorothy Gale as she clicked her ruby slipper-clad feet together. Well, the good folks of Liberal took it upon themselves to designate a house from 1907 as Miss Gale's official residence, and the place now serves as the gateway to an animatronic attraction dubbed the Land of Oz.

*QUICK FACT*

Dorothy's House features an exact replica of her room as depicted in the movie.

## S. P. Dinsmoor's Garden of Eden

***Lucas, Kansas***

A populist, schoolteacher, and veteran of the Civil War, Samuel Perry Dinsmoor started building his log cabin out of limestone "timber" because of the lack of trees. Once the cabin was finished, Dinsmoor migrated into the medium of cement and fashioned more than 2,000 sacks of the stuff into his own personal "Garden of Eden," a menagerie of oddly engaging political and religious imagery. The place faded after its creator died in 1932, but was restored in the 1970s and is now listed on the National Register of Historic Places. Tours are available year-round.

## Carhenge

***Alliance, Nebraska***

Carhenge, the funky automotive version of England's mystical stone circle, emerged in 1987 from a plan that had as much to do with remembrance as it did with art. Built to memorialize the passing of artist Jim Reinders's father, Carhenge features a circle of 38 cars that were planted and balanced upon each other to precisely replicate Stonehenge.

The end result is part Druid, part Detroit, and undeniably wacky. In keeping with the original monoliths, all cars have been spray-painted a stonelike grey. This produces the proper look even as it staves off rust.

## A Land of Henges

Feeding off the mystery of Stonehenge—the iconic Druid stones located in merry olde England—a number of American "henges" have made an appearance.

While it mimics the names of Carhenge and Stonehenge, Truckhenge *(right)* has little to do with mysticism, high art, or time telling and much to do with one man's dissatisfaction with local government.

When "artist" Ron Lessman was ordered by Shawnee County officials to "pick up" his collection of old trucks, pick them up he did. He planted six trucks at absurd angles around his grounds and festooned them with colorful protest blurbs featuring such items as, "If these trucks can't stand, why do we fight the Taliban?" and "Rome didn't kill Jesus, bureaucrats did."

*Truckhenge in Topeka, Kansas*

*Foamhenge in Natural Bridge, Virginia*

Fined $750 for his disobedience, the artist/activist remained unfazed. "Lawrence ain't worth much then, is it?" he quipped to officials.

Aside from the fact that the vehicles protrude from the ground, the arrangement bears little resemblance to the other "henges." Still, there's no denying Truckhenge's weirdness factor. For us, that's really quite enough.

In addition to Carhenge and Truckhenge, there's Foamhenge *(left)*. As its name suggests, this structure is constructed entirely of foam. In this case, the foam is Styrofoam, and its resemblance to Stonehenge is striking. Says creator Marc Cline: "It took the Druids 1,500 years to build Stonehenge. I can do it in ten days." Let's chalk it up to American ingenuity.

## Harold Warp's Pioneer Village

***Minden, Nebraska***

Judging by its name, you might expect to find Conestoga wagons and mock-ups of the Oregon Trail featured here, but pioneering covers far more than any one period. It's a fact not lost on Harold Warp. With Pioneer Village, the collector attempts to cover the span of time from 1830–1962, a span that ranks among the most fruitful in American history.

After making his fortune in plastics, Warp had the means to acquire some 50,000 artifacts but needed a place to showcase them. He accomplished this with 28 separate buildings and more than 100,000 square feet of display space.

Inside, visitors will find an eclectic hodgepodge of Americana including a frontier fort, a general store, art collections, historic flying machines, antique tractors and automobiles, atomic power displays—pretty much anything and everything that helped bring America to its present point.

Does the collection include a Conestoga wagon, the overland vehicle that opened up the West? You bet your pioneering spirit it does!

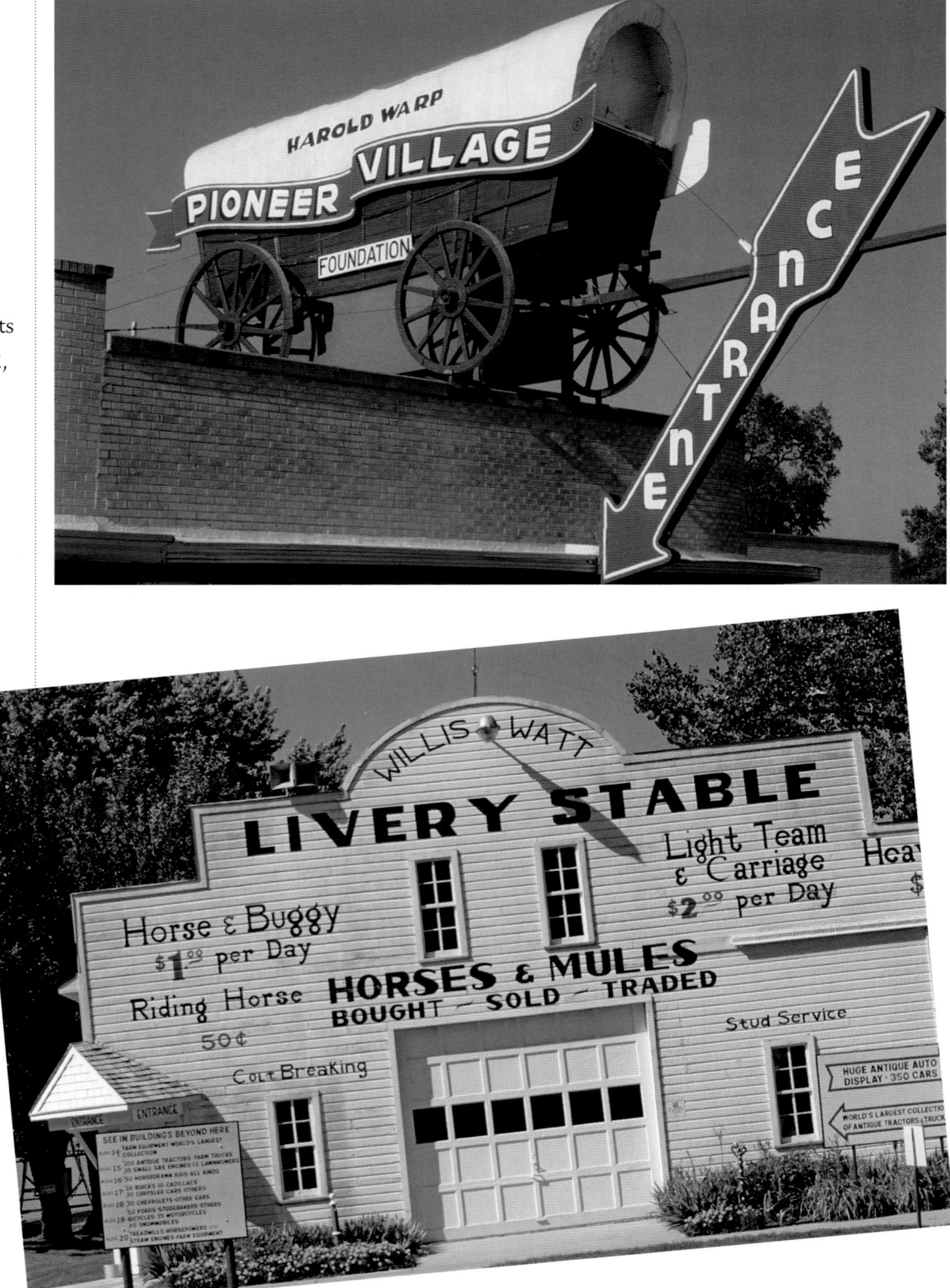

*Exhibits at Harold Warp's Pioneer Village include antique tractors and automobiles.*

## Concrete USS *South Dakota*

### *Sioux Falls, South Dakota*

As we learned with New Jersey's SS *Atlantus* (see page 74) and other floating "deadweights," concrete ships don't fare too well on the high seas. So it's a good thing the concrete USS *South Dakota* is permanently dry-docked.

Actually, that's somewhat misleading. The proud battleship was once a svelte, classy vessel made from steel. Her concrete overcoat came only *after* she was decommissioned and turned into a memorial.

But that too is misleading. Here's the scuttlebutt: In 1962, the USS *South Dakota* was scrapped. When her home state decided to memorialize her, instead of transporting the entire vessel to Sioux Falls, they kept a few guns, her propeller, anchor, and bell. Not enough to replicate an entire ship, you say? It is if you lay down a fake foot-high concrete outline and plant the genuine items in it.

The end result is a funky-looking "ship" that's part grassland, part armament, and totally strange. At 680 feet long, the unusual hybrid confounds, amuses, and memorializes. Only in America.

## National Presidential Wax Museum

***Keystone, South Dakota***

Situated just above Mount Rushmore, the National Presidential Wax Museum features all 43 presidents and includes major scenes from history. Here's President Franklin Delano Roosevelt at Yalta, there are the signers of the Declaration of Independence. You get the idea. A more recent exhibit pays homage to 9/11 and features President George W. Bush and a firefighter standing on the debris pile at "Ground Zero."

**QUICK FACT**

As if the waxed figures of past presidents weren't scary enough, the museum also features Holy Terror Mini-Golf on its grounds.

## Dinosaur Park

***Rapid City, South Dakota***

After Mount Rushmore was completed, the area around the monument experienced an economic boom. This was particularly true of Rapid City, a settlement of note sitting just to its north.

Yet Dinosaur Park, a Rapid City attraction featuring full-scale replicas of our planet's prehistoric inhabitants, has never charged a dime for admission. What gives? The truth is that Dinosaur Park represents the height of civility in a decidedly uncivilized world. Come again?

The idea for Dinosaur Park was concocted by the city and the Works Progress Administration (WPA) during the Great Depression. While the park aimed to educate and entertain with its seven dinosaur displays, it would do so only as a byproduct. Putting unemployed men back to work was its central mission.

On May 22, 1936, huge dinosaurs joined equally huge presidents in the Black Hills region. They are still standing there today, looking a bit cartoonlike, but the big fellows have nevertheless accomplished their task. After all, they spared their hardworking re-creators the incivility of a breadline. Thanks, T-Rex.

## Wall Drug

***Wall, South Dakota***

Perhaps one of the more mainstream attractions within these covers, Wall Drug nevertheless deserves its ink. Apparently its owners agree, having plastered colorful Wall Drug billboards along a 500-mile stretch of I-90 from Minnesota to Montana. Each promises weary travelers an oasis of fun, food, and shopping just ahead.

There's good reason for this. Wall Drug isn't so much a drugstore as a grand happening. Out in the South Dakota hinterlands, where the people and entertainment are sparse, such diversions are as treasured as water in the desert.

And speaking of water, it was simple $H_2O$ that really got the ball rolling for this fun-time establishment. But that's getting a bit ahead of things. Here's the backstory.

Wall Drug started on its path to commercial immortality back in 1931, when it was acquired by pharmacist Ted Hustead. Since it was located in an absurdly small town of just more than 300 residents and an economic depression was underway, the store's sales were less than stellar. Then, out of the blue, Ted's wife Dorothy seized upon an idea. Since thirst was a constant along the dusty roads of the region, Wall Drug would advertise free ice water to parched travelers. The gimmick worked. In no time, the Husteads saw a steady flow of customers. This translated to increased profits, which were then funneled into expansion, and Wall Drug—the happening—was created.

So, just what's at this place? Actually, what *isn't* here might be a more fitting question. Wall Drug includes a roaring T-Rex dinosaur; a miniature version of Mount Rushmore; an area to mine, pan, and dig for gold; a westward discovery show; a teepee; a stagecoach; a picnic area; a food

### A Jacka-what?

Wondering what a jackalope is? Well, for starters, it's not a real animal. Best to clear that up right away, as natives of the West like to have a little fun with tourists who might not realize there's no such thing. This mythical creature is purported to be a cross between a jackrabbit and an antelope. Believers interested in pursuing the sport can obtain a jackalope-hunting license in Douglas, Wyoming—the self-proclaimed "Jackalope Capital of the World" (page 252).

A giant, fiberglass jackalope stands sentry in the Back Yard.

shop; an art gallery; a jackalope display; an emporium; a chapel; a western boot and clothing store; a souvenir stand; and many, many more tourist lures. They even sell aspirin and prescriptions to anyone still interested in drug items. Crazy, huh?

These days, the enterprise still offers free ice water to thirsty travelers, and people keep right on coming. And why shouldn't they? As a much-welcomed respite from the long, boring road, the new, improved Wall Drug is simply without peer. A kazillion billboards can't be wrong!

At Wall Drug, strange and wonderful attractions fill every nook and cranny.

## Mitchell Corn Palace

***Mitchell, South Dakota***

There aren't many American travel guides that overlook the Mitchell Corn Palace. While this may sound like it qualifies the attraction for mainstream status, we assure you it does not. After all, how many buildings do you know of that you can actually eat?

The original "Corn Belt Exposition" went up in 1892. It became an impromptu chamber of commerce, and proud farmers would display their best crops on the exterior of the building. Over the years the plantings continued. A grand tradition had begun.

These days, the third corn expo (now called the Mitchell Corn Palace) acts as a living canvas and features artful murals made from corn, grasses, straw, wheat, and other tasty bits extracted from good mother Earth.

An enormous festival is held at the Corn Palace each year. It brings national-level entertainment into Mitchell and kicks off a new design for the murals and panels. In 2007–2008, "Everyday Heroes" was chosen as a theme. It celebrated teachers, doctors, parents, crossing guards, social workers—basically anyone and everyone who has made a difference in our world.

Inside the Corn Palace, people do what they usually do in large spaces. From sporting events to stage shows, the ornate building proves it can entertain even as it continues to "grow."

QUICK FACT

It takes thousands of bushels of grasses, straw, wheat, and—of course—corn to produce the murals that adorn the Corn Palace.

## Salem Sue/World's Largest Holstein Cow

***New Salem, North Dakota***

With 50-foot-tall men and women running amok throughout America (not to mention this book), you may be wondering where they get their milk. Well, wonder no more. Salem Sue, a fiberglass bovine of mind-boggling proportions, is "udderly" the best when it comes to milk production. She should be. Her belly is larger than a milk truck!

Sue is 38 feet tall by 50 feet long and visible for some five miles. Erected in 1974 by the New Salem Lions Club, the "big moo" was designed to promote Holstein herds. One can only imagine how well she does this since she's fully visible to busy I-94 traffic.

You may be wondering who milks the "grand dame of the barnyard." It's a tall order, but we're guessing the Lions Club provides this service. In fact, it appears that they've been "milking" her since 1974. Moo!

## Enchanted Highway

***Regent, North Dakota***

Pheasants on the Prairie *(1996)*

When it comes to "sizable" art, Gary Greff is without peer. The former schoolteacher, who is completely untrained in art and engineering, decided to undertake both to put his town on the map. What he ultimately built must be seen to be believed.

Greff's great works stand alongside a 32-mile road now dubbed the Enchanted Highway. There, visitors will find what are billed as the world's largest steel sculptures. The claim may actually be true. At 110 feet tall and 154 feet long, Gary's *Geese in Flight* leads that vaunted category in the *Guinness World Records*.

Then there's *Grasshopper's Delight*. If you recall the 1950s flick *Them* (where radiation-tainted ants grow huge and threaten the world), you sort of get the picture. Just replace the ants with a 40-foot-tall grasshopper and start running for shelter.

On a somewhat calmer note, observe *Theodore Roosevelt Rides Again*. In this sculpture, the famed "Rough Rider" barely controls a rearing horse. Nevertheless, "Teddy" manages to raise one hand in triumph, perhaps signaling that the West will soon be won. As with all of Greff's sculptures, this 51-foot-tall offering required the help of many volunteers.

In addition to this trio, four more whimsical sculptures loom large along the

Grasshopper's Delight *(1999)*

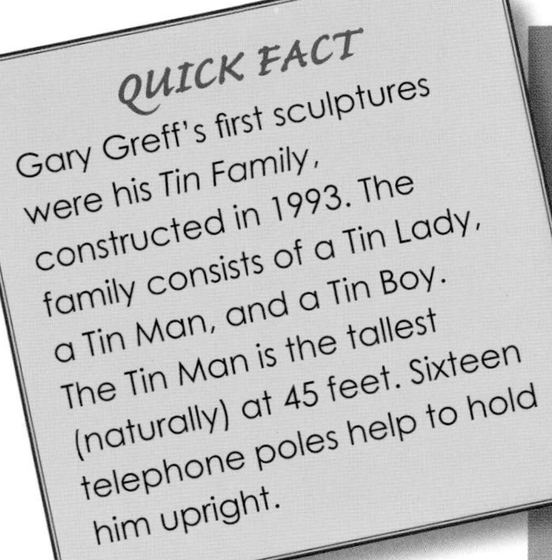

QUICK FACT

Gary Greff's first sculptures were his Tin Family, constructed in 1993. The family consists of a Tin Lady, a Tin Man, and a Tin Boy. The Tin Man is the tallest (naturally) at 45 feet. Sixteen telephone poles help to hold him upright.

Enchanted Highway. All are made from discarded items, and all appear to have been created by a fine, seasoned artist. But then Gary Greff *is* a fine, seasoned artist. It's just that his seasoning is rather new.

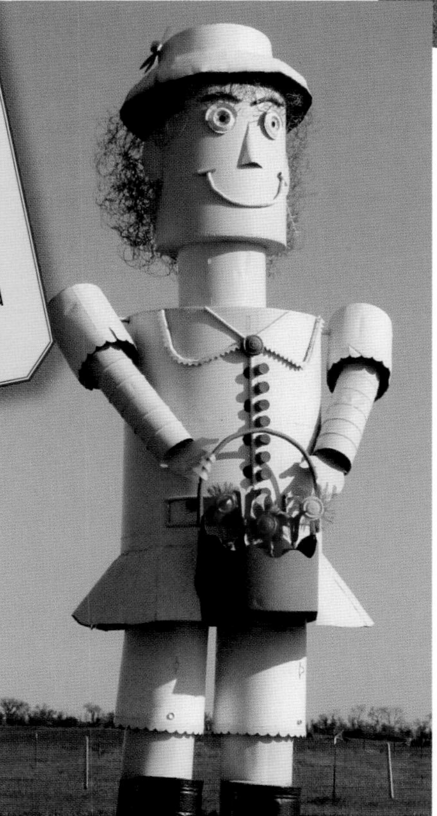

Tin Family *(1993)*

# W'eel Turtle

***Dunseith, North Dakota***

Made from 2,000 tire rims that never made it to their destination, W'eel stands sentinel on the North Dakota prairie and lures customers to Dale's Thrifty Barn, the gas station/café/motel responsible for its existence. The 40-foot turtle's one-ton head bobs from side to side, perhaps acknowledging the surrounding Turtle Mountains.

## Fargo Walk of Fame

***Fargo, North Dakota***

A hand and foot up on the competition? That's what Fargo businessman Mike Stevens seemed to be thinking when he devised the Fargo Walk of Fame.

Patterned after the famous walkway outside of Grauman's (now Mann's) Chinese Theatre in Los Angeles, the walk contains more than 100 celebrity signatures, handprints, and footprints.

It's almost as if Fargo is throwing down the gauntlet and issuing Hollywood a challenge. With stars such as Garth Brooks, KISS, Neil Diamond, and Tiny Tim doing the Fargo plaster act, the west coast star-factory had better beware. Bollywood (India's movie industry) is already nipping at Hollywood's toes. Can Fargo's *Follywood* be far behind?

# Chapter Five
# THE SOUTHWEST

When the sun sets in these parts, it illuminates pink and blue canyons, crimson red mesas, imposing buttes, and purple mountains so beautiful they can bring tears to one's eyes.

With such beauty acting as a lure, it's not surprising that the region is a favorite of artists. Many have chosen to dwell here so they can tap into such inspiration.

Wherever mainstream artists congregate, you'll usually find an eccentric fringe. Don't take that the wrong way; "eccentric" is a *good* thing. This is particularly true here in the Southwest, where whimsical artists have given us such offbeat offerings as Thunder Mountain in Imlay, Nevada, and the Toilet Seat Art Museum in Alamo Heights, Texas. The Burning Man and Whole Enchilada festivals prove that the Southwest's populace is every bit as offbeat as its artists. We'd expect nothing less.

*Burning Man Festival,*
*Black Rock Desert, Nevada*

## Neon Museum

***Las Vegas, Nevada***

Does anything adorn the night sky more strikingly than a colorful neon sign? It's obvious how supporters of Las Vegas's Neon Museum feel about the question. Within a designated area at the intersection of Las Vegas Boulevard and Fremont Street (known as the Fremont Street Experience), the colorful icons that first put Las Vegas on the map are kept buzzing. And we do mean *buzzing*.

When casinos and businesses shut down, their glitzy neon signs were kept in the Young Electric Sign Company's "boneyard" awaiting an uncertain fate. When natural elements appeared to be taking a toll, the Neon Museum stepped in and restored many of them.

Today, visitors can see enormous signs lifted from classic Vegas hotels such as the Golden Nugget and the Silver Slipper, and marvel at the multicolors of the Hacienda Horse and Rider and Binion's Horseshoe. "What happens in Vegas stays in Vegas," the saying goes. In the case of the giant neon signs and the paternal organization that oversees them, we hope the adage holds true.

## Madame Tussauds Las Vegas

***Las Vegas, Nevada***

Laid out much like a cocktail party, Madame Tussauds Las Vegas gets fans up close and personal with the "beautiful people." Wax icons of celebrities such as Cher, Sean Connery, Bette Midler, Marilyn Monroe, and scores of others stand around just waiting to meet the flotsam and jetsam (um, that's you and me) of society.

With more than 100 wax figures holding court, a fan is never far from a star. Pictures taken beside the figures can easily fool people into believing a genuine meeting took place. Just don't be annoyed by the stars' apparent snootiness. When asked for their autographs, not one of these Hollywood figures answered our request.

**QUICK FACT**

Interactive exhibits offer once-in-a-lifetime photo opportunities. When else will you get to ride alongside Evel Knievel or marry George Clooney?

## Thunder Mountain

***Imlay, Nevada***

Folk artist Frank Van Zant built Thunder Mountain over a 21-year period beginning in 1968, then promptly committed suicide. The impetus for his untimely exit is unknown. Better documented are Van Zant's reasons for building Thunder Mountain.

According to newspapers, an old medicine woman told Van Zant, "In the final days there shall rise up a place called Thunder Mountain." She further explained that only those living there would survive the apocalypse. Van Zant changed his name to Chief Rolling Mountain Thunder and got busy. *Real* busy.

Using an assortment of discarded bottles, tools, auto parts, wood bits, car windshields, railroad ties, and other items, the Chief built a Native American tribute "mountain" that boggles the mind.

Some three stories tall, the display sits in full view of I-80 and causes many weary travelers to question their sanity. From an in-your-face "Naked Man" statue to some 200 sculptures of faces and figures, the mountain is an eclectic compilation of anything and everything.

*These folk art sculptures offer just a taste of what visitors will discover during a visit to Thunder Mountain.*

## Burning Man Festival
***Black Rock Desert, Nevada***

Anyone who still views Woodstock as the gold standard for mass self-expression has probably not attended the annual Burning Man Festival in Nevada's Black Rock Desert. Those that *have* attended already know just how weird things can get out there in "Black Rock City," the name conferred upon this temporary desert community of 50,000. With daytime temps that routinely break 100 degrees, followed by nights that sometimes dip below the freezing mark, attendees have every right to feel disoriented.

Burning Man, while essentially an art festival, embodies the spirit of a Woodstock-style gathering. Held each year one week before and straight through the Labor Day weekend, the event finds attendees pitching "survival" tents, carting in huge quantities of life-sustaining $H_2O$, and living by rules of self-sufficiency.

Creators Larry Harvey and Jerry James dig "happenings"—particularly ones that feature the in-your-face art of radical self-expression. In 1986, they and others met on San Francisco's Baker Beach to celebrate the summer solstice. For reasons shrouded in mystery, this inaugural event included an eight-foot-tall "man" burned in effigy. It was an instant hit.

Progressively larger men were systematically torched until 1990 when police extinguished the fun. It was this turn of events that led to the Burning Man Festival's relocation to Nevada's Black Rock Desert.

The big guy has been doing "burnouts" here ever since.

Burning Man's central theme is its art. Creations range from "art cars" festooned to resemble giant insects to psychedelic steel sculptures of whirligigs and transformerlike objects. Tents house more traditional canvas art in its many and varied forms. One never knows what bizarre thing they'll see next, and the search is half the fun. Exhibits include forms of artistic self-expression such as mass nudism and public displays of absurdity. Audience participation *is* the sideshow at Burning Man, and much like our world, it's forever in a state of flux.

Not surprisingly, the biggest moment arrives six days into the event when the Burning Man himself is set ablaze and fried to a crisp. At 40 feet tall, the nighttime conflagration can be seen for miles across the table-flat desert landscape.

*Art is part of the experience at Burning Man. Participants are encouraged to interact with the exhibits.*

## Giant Prospector

***Washoe Valley, Nevada***

This 20-foot-tall fiberglass prospector brandishes an oversize chunk of faux gold in order to attract chocoholics to the Chocolate Nugget Candy Factory, located between Reno and Carson City on U.S. 395. Before his stint hocking candy, he was the mascot of a casino in nearby Sparks.

## Whole Enchilada Festival

***Las Cruces, New Mexico***

Like many annual festivals, Las Cruces's Whole Enchilada Festival is a multiday get-together aimed at mirth and merriment. Unlike other events, this one also features the creation of the World's Largest Enchilada.

To accomplish this grand culinary feat, 750 pounds of stone-ground corn dough are pressed into one bodacious tortilla. The flat bread is then carted off by a team of workers and mated with 175 gallons of vegetable oil.

Next, 175 pounds of grated cheese and 50 pounds of chopped onions are added. This is topped off by 75 gallons of red chile sauce. The procedure is duplicated two more times and stacked layer to layer. Attendees are given a green light, and the feast commences. Past festivals have attracted as many as 40,000 people. Heartburn statistics have never been recorded.

QUICK FACT
From beginning to end, the enchilida-making process takes two-and-a-half hours.

# Tinkertown Museum

***Sandia Park, New Mexico***

Tinkertown is an Old West frontier town come to life—in miniature, that is. It contains carved wooden figures that were originally part of a traveling exhibit. Somehow, some way, these mini-mites banded together and formed their own town.

Old West storefronts lead to a world taken over by raucous miniature inhabitants. These include circus performers that challenge tigers and defy gravity and "Otto the One-Man-Band," who serenades visitors as they walk along.

Tinkertown was constructed over a 40-year period by Ross Ward. Its 22 rooms feature eccentric collections of Americana that offer up more than a little fun. For a quarter, Esmeralda the Fortune Teller will predict your destiny. If it proves to be less than stellar, a second stroll past Otto is likely in order.

*A quirky wooden band provides a glimpse of the wonderful oddities housed in Tinkertown.*

*A small section of the rambling walls that surround the museum.*

**QUICK FACT**

The walls of this 22-room museum are made up of 50,000 glass bottles.

## Roswell UFO Festival

***Roswell, New Mexico***

As far as alleged government cover-ups go, there isn't a bigger dog in the land than the Roswell UFO incident. On July 7, 1947, eyewitness sightings led many to believe that a UFO crash-landed at a ranch near Roswell, New Mexico. Official military reports denied an alien crash (cue mysterious music) and maintained that an ordinary weather balloon had simply met its end. When this and other UFO encounters are studied, the "official" reports generally try to discredit the possibility that UFOs have been encountered. Resulting speculation has run rampant and turned once-anonymous Roswell into UFO central.

From lectures to music, spaceship mock-ups to conspiracy-mongering, the annual four-day Roswell UFO Festival strives to educate as it entertains.

Lectures and seminars take place at the respected International UFO Museum, while other less formal extraterrestrial "statements" pop up just about everywhere throughout town. Many of these blur the line between UFO science and sheer madness, but probably account for a good deal of the festival's popularity. After all, if visitors were seeking "normal," they wouldn't be coming to Roswell in the first place.

Despite thousands of annual attendees and umpteen meetings where information is exchanged, the festival hasn't turned up much in regards to the original incident. But that small detail doesn't seem to matter to UFO aficionados. Whether pro or con on the question of a government cover-up, all agree that something mighty strange occurred here more than a half-century ago. The implication fires the imagination as it fills the seats.

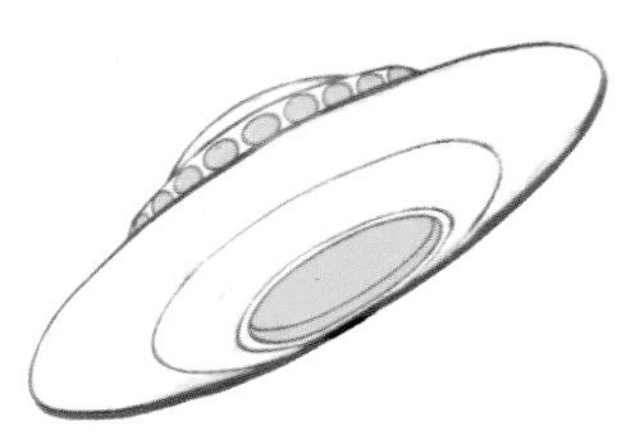

**QUICK FACT**
Festival entertainment includes Fourth of July fireworks and an alien costume contest.

## Blue Whale

***Catoosa, Oklahoma***

A surviving icon along historic U.S. Route 66, the smiling blue whale tells quite a tale.

Hoping to show wife Zelta (a collector of whale figurines) a whale of a good time for their wedding anniversary, Hugh Davis constructed the blue giant out of pipe and concrete in the early 1970s.

Built over a spring-fed pond, the whale features a slide and a mouth so large it could swallow people whole. Eventually, word of the great beast spread, and Davis commercialized the operation. A sandy beach, picnic tables, and lifeguards now welcomed would-be "Captain Ahabs" interested in a refreshing dip.

Everything went swimmingly at the "Fun and Swim Blue Whale" until 1988 when the attraction went belly-up. In short order, nature began to reclaim the site.

In 2000, concerned Catoosa citizens stepped in and restored the whale. While no longer operated as a swimming concession, the blue whale continues to trigger double takes from nostalgic Route 66 travelers. And that's no fish story.

## World's Largest Concrete Totem Pole

***Foyil, Oklahoma***

If the thought of beholding the World's Largest *Concrete* Totem Pole gets your engine running, beat a hasty retreat to Foyil, Oklahoma, home of Ed Galloway's Totem Pole Park.

It took Galloway (who was "looking for something to do") 11 years, adding one bucket of cement at a time, to create the centerpiece to his park. Finished in 1948, the 90-foot-tall tribute to Native American culture has more than 200 different carvings on its facade, and its base is a stout 18 feet in diameter. It is adorned with owls, spirit lizards, and Indian chiefs.

The totem pole rests on the back of a colorful—and hardy!—concrete turtle.

QUICK FACT
Noodling is the subject of a one-hour documentary titled Okie Noodling (2001).

## Okie Catfish Noodling Tournament

***Paul's Valley, Oklahoma***

Noodling involves catching a catfish with one's bare hands. *Really.*

The annual Okie Catfish Noodling Tournament pits crafty humans against equally cagey fish. With the aid of a "spotter," a noodler dives underwater to depths approaching 20 feet to retrieve his quarry, which are usually hiding out under rocks. With winning specimens weighing as much as 50 to 60 pounds, this is no small feat.

The 24-hour tournament started in 2000. Noodlers are permitted to catch their prey in any body of water statewide but must bring their catch to a central point for weighing. Afterward, cheers and jeers are exchanged, and noodlers set their sights on the next contest, often lamenting "the one that got away."

## Golden Driller

***Tulsa, Oklahoma***

Originally erected for the International Petroleum Exposition in 1953, the Golden Driller claims the title of World's Largest Freestanding Statue—76 feet tall and 43,500 pounds. The big guy was refurbished and relocated to his current home at the Tulsa Exposition Center in 1966, where he has since survived tornadoes, art critics, and even the occasional shotgun blast.

The Golden Driller rests his hand on a real oil derrick used in an oil field in Seminole, Oklahoma. The towering statue stands in tribute to "the men of the petroleum industry who by their vision and daring have created from God's abundance a better life for mankind" (inscription on plaque at the base of the statue).

**QUICK FACT**

In 1979, the state legislature named the Golden Driller Oklahoma's state monument.

## Devil's Rope Barbed Wire Museum

***McLean, Texas***

Think you've seen it all? Then you're obviously not familiar with the Devil's Rope Barbed Wire Museum. This is one offbeat place.

This "sharp" display is located on old Route 66 and traces the history of barbed-wire fencing.

How many are aware that Joseph F. Glidden of DeKalb, Illinois, invented barbed wire? Or that this cattle-containing wire helped develop the West? The museum tells you more than you probably need to know about barbed wire, but therein lies its fun factor.

Luckily, the museum has seen fit to keep its spikiest specimens behind glass. That's what we call sharp thinking.

Did you know that barbed wire was once dubbed the "Devil's Rope" by religious groups? It's true. When livestock first encountered the wire, they would let out quite a yelp. The faithful surmised that only the devil could be behind such a torturous item, hence the colorful moniker.

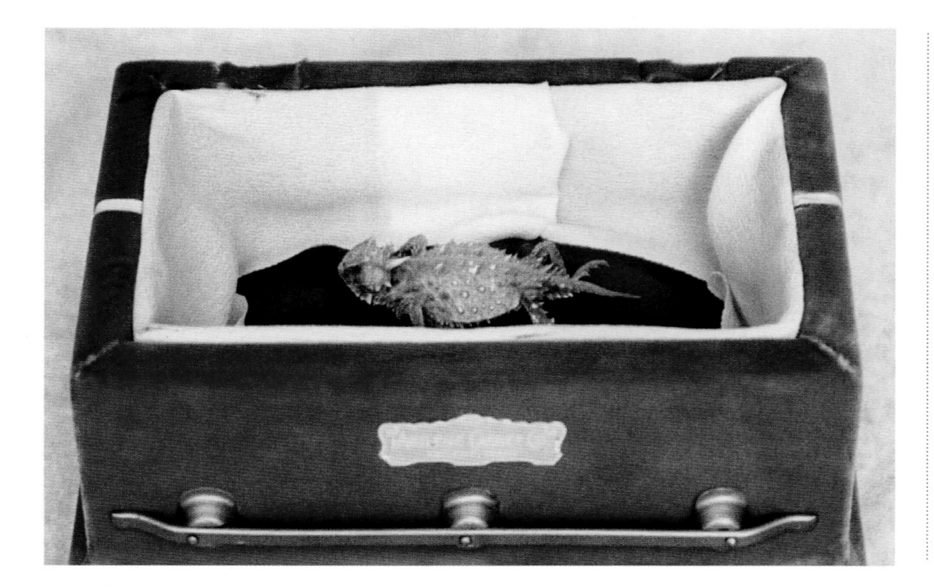

## Old Rip

***Eastland, Texas***

Built in 1897, the Eastland County Courthouse in northern Texas had a legend living in its cornerstone until the wrecking ball came calling in 1928. Defying all biological explanation, a horned toad somehow lived to see daylight after dwelling in the cornerstone for 31 years. Hoax or not, locals dubbed the reptile "Old Rip" (after Rip Van Winkle) and took him on tour. The famous toad even met President Calvin Coolidge. He passed away soon thereafter and has called the new Eastland County Courthouse home ever since: His embalmed body is on display under glass.

## Cockroach Hall of Fame

***Plano, Texas***

Before you depart this big blue marble called Earth, you owe yourself a few chuckles. That's where pest control specialist Michael Bohdan comes in. He dressed up a number of creepy, crawly cockroaches, placed them in themed dioramas, and started a museum.

Famous types of every crawl make an appearance at the offbeat attraction (which also doubles as the business address for Bohdan's retail store). Have a laugh with comic David Letter*roach* or enjoy a piano concerto by Libe*roach*i. How about a visit to *Roach* Liberty, where the famous statue lifts her *roach* beside the golden door?

Perhaps the strangest bug is the one that welcomes unwary visitors to the Combates Motel. As a takeoff on the movie *Psycho*, the white-wigged roach wields a knife and slides along a track between the motel and a spooky house. In this creepy scenario, it's the humans who check in but don't check out. Ah, sweet revenge!

**QUICK FACT**

Do you have a bug phobia? Never fear—most of the roaches at this museum are dead. However, Bohdan does have some live Madagascar hissing cockroaches for your viewing pleasure.

# Forbidden Gardens

### *Katy, Texas*

Why travel all the way to China to experience its wonders when a nifty replica exists in Katy, Texas? The $20-million outdoor attraction features such Chinese staples (in miniature) as the Forbidden City of Beijing, the Temple of Heaven, and the Calming of the Heart Lodge.

Tranquil Chinese music, courtyards, and Koi fish ponds add to the illusion, while a 6,000-piece terra-cotta army (in one-third scale) reminds visitors that things weren't quite so serene in the third century B.C. Spread out over 40 acres, the Forbidden Gardens covers some 2,000 years of Chinese history. That this attraction exists on the Texas flatlands only adds to its mystery and allure.

*Emperor Quin surveys his army of 6,000.*

*The terra-cotta soldiers are intricately detailed.*

*The chariot is one of many elaborate replicas to be found in the Forbidden Gardens.*

*The terra-cotta army at the gate keeps the peace in this tranquil courtyard.*

# Toilet Seat Art Museum

***Alamo Heights, Texas***

Self-proclaimed "toilet seat artist" Barney Smith has created more than 700 unique toilet seat works and placed them in his garage-turned-museum for viewing. As a retired master plumber, Smith knows commode lids better than just about anyone.

More than 30 years ago, Smith modified his first toilet seat when he used one to mount a set of deer antlers. From that point forward, Smith has been "sitting down on the job," so to speak.

His creations include license plate seats; tribute seats; Elks, Lions Club, and Rotary seats; seats that feature cutlery, pens, and fragrances; and a whole slew of other crazy toilet-art pieces.

## National Museum of Funeral History

***Houston, Texas***

We all have to go sometime. If founder Robert L. Waltrip has his way, our destination will be the National Museum of Funeral History in Houston, Texas.

This vast, 20,000-square-foot museum is packed to the rafters with caskets, coffins, hearses, and other items that relate in some way to the death process.

Opened in 1992 as a way to honor "one of our most important cultural rituals," the scope of the operation is impressive, as are some of its more unusual exhibits.

A real "crowd" pleaser comes in the form of a 1916 Packard Funeral Bus. This bizarre vehicle seems to ask, "Why deal with long funeral processions when this baby can do it all?" Designed to carry a coffin, pallbearers, and up to 20 mourners, the bus was retired after it tipped over during a San Francisco funeral in 1952, ejecting mourners *and* the mourned into the street.

Rather playfully, a sign in the museum reads, "Any day above ground is a good one." In general, we agree. But after checking out the museum's ultra-cool fantasy coffins, "six feet under" doesn't seem all *that* bad.

*The museum's fantasy coffin display shows the lighter side of being six feet under.*

*A collection of hearses offers a historical perspective into the funeral industry.*

## Hutto Hippos

***Hutto, Texas***

Driving through Hutto, Texas, one thing quickly becomes apparent: Hutto is hippopotamus country. In fact, Hutto reveres the enormous beast like none other. How do they show their affection for the ungainly mammal? By distributing hippo statues virtually everywhere.

An exhibit called "Hippo Lure" explains how an old circus train once passed through town. When a hippo broke loose and wandered to Cottonwood Creek, the town had a new mascot.

Today, visitors will find a Lone Star Hippo, a Stars and Stripes Hippo, a Texas Longhorn Hippo, and a Hippo Crossing among other hippopotami. There's even a stationary 725-pound concrete hippo that's designed to be "ridden." Just the thing for a safari on the cheap.

**QUICK FACT**

In 2003, the Texas state legislature named Hutto the Hippo Capital of Texas.

**QUICK FACT**

Pranksters sometimes paint nail polish or knee socks on the sculpture, but these adornments are quickly sandblasted off the legs. Still, you never know what you might find here. Perhaps your next visit will sock it to you with another surprise?

## Ozymandias Leg Ruins

***Amarillo, Texas***

The Ozymandias Leg Ruins were inspired by a Percy Bysshe Shelley poem titled "Ozymandias." The statue's appearance suggests that it was once an entire body (it never was), and a fictional historical marker suggests that students from Lubbock destroyed it.

## Orange Show Monument

***Houston, Texas***

Built by folk artist and postal worker Jefferson Davis McKissack, the Orange Show Monument pays homage to one of America's most beloved fruits.

McKissack erected his 3,000-square-foot shrine to citrus between 1956 and 1979. For building materials, he used such things as concrete, steel, and brick. For adornments, the junk man came to the rescue with discarded tiles, wagon wheels, tractor seats, old mannequins, and statuettes.

Sporting an orange-and-white color scheme, the monument features educational boards that tout the orange's many benefits. An oasis, wishing well, pond, stage, museum, and gift shop all provide a nifty backdrop for McKissack's favorite fruit.

## Art Car Parade

When McKissack died in 1980, a nonprofit organization calling itself the Orange Show Foundation stepped in to preserve his monument. In 1988, the group commissioned a display of mobile art they called the Fruitmobile. And this is how the celebration known as the Art Car Parade was born. At the Houston Art Car parade, artists get to show off their idiosyncrasies in a mobile medium. The parade features wacky cars that make vehicles from *Mad Max* appear almost ordinary.

Take, for example, the Hen-A-Tron II, a hen/car hybrid that represents the type of auto lunacy that prevails at the parade. From here, the asphalt is the limit.

Past parade entries have included a Volkswagen Beetle with another upside-down Beetle welded to its roof *(below)*, a Sunflower car where driver and friends sit high in an elevated sun pod, and a giant Gold Star car that looks to be uncontrollable. Each year the entries get more artistic, more intricate, and dare we say, weirder. Bravo!

**QUICK FACT**

The first parade included some 40 cars. Today's parade showcases more than 250 vehicles and is not limited to cars. Anything with wheels—bicycles, lawn mowers, and so forth—can participate.

## World's Largest Killer Bee

***Hidalgo, Texas***

While "Killer Bee Capital of the World" doesn't sound like a moniker that will attract many out-of-towners, Hidalgo has embraced the title and gone a step further by building a 20-foot-long stinger outside city hall. The city nabbed the title after the country's first killer bee colony was discovered nearby in 1990.

QUICK FACT
If you're trying to avoid the sting of a killer bee, better put on your running shoes. These aggressive insects have been known to pursue their prey for up to a quarter of a mile.

## World's Largest Rattlesnake

***Freer, Texas***

Poised to strike visitors to the Freer Chamber of Commerce, this menacing reptile replica commemorates the annual Freer Rattlesnake Round-up, a yearly festival that began in the 1960s. The event itself is also dubbed a world's largest (although the folks behind the rattlesnake round-up in Sweetwater, Texas, beg to differ).

## Rattlesnake Bridge

***Tucson, Arizona***

While most desert residents look at a rattlesnake with fear, dread, or both, transportation planners in Tucson decided to grab the serpent by the tail and dare pedestrians to shake free of their phobias. Snaking over busy Broadway, the Rattlesnake Bridge is actually a piece of functional art—a two-lane walking and biking bridge, complete with noisemaking rattle—that's growing on the locals. The bridge has been voted Best Public Art a few times by *Tucson Weekly* readers beginning in 2003.

## Meteor Crater

***Winslow, Arizona***

**QUICK FACT**

When a meteor travels through Earth's atmosphere, it is heated to very high temperatures. The heat usually causes a lot of the meteor to melt away. However, some meteors are so large that they hit the earth as meteorites, leaving a large impact crater behind.

Talk about your collisions. When a 150-foot-wide meteorite slammed into Earth approximately 50,000 years ago, it made quite an impact. Moving at supersonic speed, the enormous rock generated an explosive force equivalent to 20 million tons of TNT and carved its place in history.

Bearing an uncanny resemblance to many of the moon's infamous pockmarks, Meteor Crater features a lifted lip some 150 feet tall and a deep-dished hole 4,000 feet in diameter by 550 feet deep.

Today, visitors walk the crater's rim and ponder the immense power of the cosmos. When the implication becomes overbearing, they buy miniature impact trinkets at the gift shop.

### A Crater by Another Name

Scientists typically refer to Meteor Crater as Barringer Crater, in honor of the man who correctly identified the crater as the impact from a meteorite. Prior to 1903, when Barringer stepped in, the large crater had been credited to volcanic activity.

## Shady Dell RV Park

***Bisbee, Arizona***

For those who'd like to step back into the good ole days, the Shady Dell RV Park offers a way. Choosing from a fleet of vintage aluminum travel trailers (including the coveted Airstream) from the 1940s and 1950s, time-travelers can relive halcyon days of yore surrounded by reassuring tidbits from the past.

Available for overnight and weekly rentals, each shiny trailer is kept as close to original as possible. To enhance the retro experience, "vintage" radios (set up to play cassettes from the big-band era as well as favorite old radio programs) are included. Trailers also feature black-and-white televisions, vintage records and phonographs, era-specific books and magazines, and outdoor barbeque grills with period lounge chairs.

To further the time-warp effect, "Dot's Diner," a restored 1957 Valentine ten-stool model, serves it up hot seven days per week. Who says you can't go back?

## Golf Ball House

***Yucca, Arizona***

Taking golf mania to the extreme, a private citizen actually lives inside this 40-foot-diameter golf ball. Even more strangely, he bought the joint *used*.

Originally slated to become a restaurant and nightclub, the project fell through, and the golf ball house landed in the rough. Enter Hank Schimmel. He and wife Ardell grabbed their irons (oodles of cash, actually) and effectively put the ball back into play.

Aside from its golf heritage, the house sports another unique feature. From certain angles, it looks just like a spaceship. With a highway situated quite close to the alien invader, we're guessing quite a few have run for the hills after seeing it. We advise against such foolhardiness and offer up this suggestion instead: Don't worry about little green men. But if someone yells "fore" near this baby, run for your life!

## Eliphante

***Cornville, Arizona***

**QUICK FACT**
So did the creators of Eliphante just really like elephants? As it turns out, they didn't set out to create an elephantlike structure. It was just a happy accident.

Built over a 28-year period starting in 1979, Eliphante would make a worthy home for a sorcerer. The brainchild of artist Michael Kahn (who passed away in 2007) and his wife Leda Livant, nothing about this living sculpture seems conventional.

Entered via an elephant-shape tunnel—hence its catchy name—Eliphante contains oddities not found in your typical tract house. The compound's living quarters, or "Hippodome," features a free-flowing kitchen countertop that grows in a bizarre spiral from wall to ceiling. In another room, a piano is built into a wall of driftwood. Walls are made from rebar and pipe coated with concrete. Attached to these are mosaics of rock, ceramics, glass, and wood. The effect is earthy and haphazard, all at once.

The latest edition to the three-acre complex is a section called "Pipedreams." Here, a labyrinth of tunnels leads to multiple art galleries featuring the abstract paintings of its creators. From this funky house, we'd expect nothing less.

QUICK FACT

You'll find most of the comforts of home in the Hippodome. The dwelling features heat, electricity, and water. There's no bathroom, though.

*Unusual doesn't begin to cover Eliphante.*

## Biosphere 2

***Oracle, Arizona***

Could human beings prosper in outer space if their house was an artificial, self-contained ecosystem? This is the question Biosphere 2 asked upon its completion in 1991.

*Space-age structures in the desert help re-create the earth's environment.*

Longer than two football fields, the fully sealed "world" became the largest such environment ever created by humans. A rainforest, mangrove swamp, ocean, Savannah grassland, and other natural features mimicked planet Earth, while a live-in crew allowed for monitoring and study of its effect on humans.

In 2006, after a plague of difficulties placed its collected data in question, the giant structure was no longer maintained as an airtight facility. Its future fell into uncertainty. Fortunately, in 2007, the University of Arizona stepped in to take over research at the Biosphere.

**QUICK FACTS**

Visitors weren't allowed inside Biosphere 2 until the year 2002, when guided tours were first offered.

In 2008, Biosphere 2 was among *USA Today*'s top 51 picks for "fresh" summer destinations.

*No need to leave the building—this rain forest is indoors!*

## Ostrich Festival

***Chandler, Arizona***

As its name suggests, this colorful annual celebration fixates on the ostrich. This is not surprising since Chandler has a rich history of ostrich ranching—an endeavor that yields stylish plumes for its troubles.

What *is* surprising is the festival's turnout. Each year, some 250,000 to 350,000 ostrich lovers attend the three-day event to observe and take part in ostrich-related activities.

Without a doubt the most popular of these are the Ostrich Races, where human beings dressed as gladiators do the Ben-Hur bit behind gangly, if surprisingly nimble, birds.

Called one of the "Top 10 Unique Festivals in the United States," the Ostrich Festival has been a Chandler staple since 1989. There's nothing at all gangly about that!

*The Ostrich Races are a popular draw at the festival.*

**QUICK FACT**

The Ostrich Festival was thrust into the spotlight when it was featured in 1995's *Waiting to Exhale*, starring Whitney Houston.

## Roy Purcell's Murals

### *Chloride, Arizona*

If a career in art is the objective, an art-rich portfolio helps to open doors. In the case of Roy Purcell, a major component of his portfolio is contained in a 2,000-square-foot section of boulders in Chloride, Arizona. Too bad they don't make briefcases this big.

In 1966, the artist took a break from college and went to work as a miner. While working among boulders, an idea hit. Why not practice his art using the rocks as his canvas?

Purcell's colorful murals include a goddess, a premonition scene, a panel called *Mandala*, and an all-encompassing mural known as *The Journey.* Since these works were largely responsible for Purcell's subsequent success in the art world, his odyssey was a path well chosen.

*Purcell's* Premonition *mural*

The Goddess *panel*

> **QUICK FACT**
> The longhorn skull is made of plaster and rebar. It measures 40 feet from horn to horn.

## Longhorn Bar & Grill

***Amado, Arizona***

It's difficult to imagine a restaurant more western than one shaped like a giant longhorn skull. That's the case at the Longhorn Grill, a desert outpost eatery located in the saguaro-studded sands between Tucson, Arizona, and Nogales, Mexico. Besides functioning as a restaurant, the building has been used as a location for several movies, including *Alice Doesn't Live Here Anymore* (1974) and *Boys on the Side* (1995).

A NOBLE
& ABSURD UNDERTAKING
I'M A

## Chapter Six

# THE ROCKY MOUNTAINS

Talk about your "rough and ready" regions. A topographic map of the Rocky Mountains looks like someone stuck all of our nation's "lumps" in one area. While that's not entirely true, the 14,000-foot-high Rocky Mountain region is, on average, one of the loftiest areas found in the lower 48 states.

With such elevation comes great hardship. Winters can be brutal throughout the region. As a result, inhabitants find themselves "holed up" for months at a time. This leads to "cabin creativity"—a condition that fuels ideas for amazing and unusual projects come springtime.

If the World's Largest Hercules Beetle in Colorado Springs, Colorado, doesn't illustrate this point clearly enough, the Dog Bark Park Inn (an inn shaped like a dog) in Cottonwood, Idaho, and the World's Largest Penguin in Cut Bank, Montana, certainly do. It's as if these highlanders have thrown down the gauntlet for offbeat supremacy. And we've all become the benefactors.

*Dog Bark Park Inn, Cottonwood, Idaho*

## Casa Bonita

***Denver, Colorado***

Interested in some dinner with a heaping side of entertainment? Head on over to Casa Bonita. Opened in 1974, this Mexican eatery screams "fiesta." From an 85-foot pink tower to a dome festooned in ornate 22-karat gold leaf, the 52,000-square-foot facility does its level best to entertain.

Diners will encounter caverns and caves, gold and silver mines, an amusement arcade, the governor's mansion, Chiquita the angry Gorilla, and a whole slew of other neat things.

Sounds like an eatery we could really sink our teeth into!

### Now That's Entertainment!

Among the entertainment offerings on the menu at Casa Bonita are cliff divers. These brave souls dive from the 30-foot-tall waterfall into a 14-foot-deep pool.

## Bishop's Castle

***Beulah, Colorado***

Another version of one man's castle fantasy come to light, this imposing offering is perhaps the largest of its kind. Construction began in 1969 and continues to this very day.

Billed by its creator as "the country's biggest 1-man project with the help of god," the fortress features a 160-foot-tall main tower flanked by turrets and gabled roofs of uncommon proportions. Builder Jim Bishop explains, "I always wanted a castle." The ambitious man hopes to complete the work before he shuffles off this mortal coil. Bishop purchased the land on which the castle is built at age 15. It cost him a little more than $1,000.

The castle is currently open to the public on a donation basis. If Bishop has his determined way, a roller coaster may someday grace the castle's walls. Imagine that.

**QUICK FACT**

Talk about the castle that has everything. Bishop even included a fire-breathing dragon in the castle's great hall.

## Coney Island

***Bailey, Colorado***

This hot dog–shape building is, not too surprisingly, a hot dog stand. While it actually began life on Colfax Avenue in Denver, it was relocated from its urban birthplace to the Rocky Mountain foothills in 1969. In 2006, the building moved again—this time to Bailey, Colorado.

**QUICK FACT**

Los Angeles, California, is also home to a hot dog–shape hot dog stand. It's called Tail o' the Pup.

QUICK FACT

The beetle is made of fiberglass and steel.

## World's Largest Hercules Beetle

***Colorado Springs, Colorado***

Built in 1958, the World's Largest Hercules Beetle lives only to evade bug spray and point the way toward the John May Natural History Museum. Given that the creature is 9 feet tall and 16 feet long, we're guessing the 400-pound bug persuades a fair share of people to continue on to the museum—or else.

## Swetsville Zoo

***Timnath, Colorado***

The Swetsville Zoo takes its name from creator Bill Swets. The zoo's steel sculptures date back as far as 1985 and run the gamut from "dinosaurs" named Tannerasaurus and Kylesaurus (after Swets's grandsons Tanner and Kyle) to "Puff," a two-headed winged dragon. The pieces are constructed from old farm equipment, discarded car parts, and other scrap materials.

Nonzoological types will be impressed by an extraterrestrial wearing cowboy boots, dejected-looking Humpty Dumpty figures, and a diminutive fellow wrestling an impossibly large fishing pole.

Occasionally asked to part with his pieces, Swets prefers making people happy to turning a profit. "This is my hobby, not my business," says Swets. In keeping with this generous spirit, admission to the zoo is free, though donations are accepted.

In May 2009, the zoo was dismantled to make room for roadway expansion. The sculptures were to be dispersed throughout the city. Others were placed in storage.

**QUICK FACT**

The Swetsville Zoo attracts as many as 20,000 visitors each year.

## Mike the Headless Chicken

***Fruita, Colorado***

The story of this attraction dates back to 1945. With an eye on the evening's dinner, Lloyd Olsen took an ax to a rooster, delivering what should have been a fatal chop. Astonishingly, the decapitated rooster (soon to be named Mike) survived. Olsen, impressed by Mike's will to live, decided to spare him and nurse him back to headless health. He accomplished this with an eyedropper filled with life-sustaining grain and water.

It was later determined that the ax had missed Mike's jugular vein, allowing the rooster to stand tall. He'd make it a full 18 months before finally succumbing.

Today, a 300-pound, 5-foot-tall version of the rooster stands as a fitting memorial to Mike—the little rooster that could.

**QUICK FACT**

An annual festival is held the third weekend in May to celebrate Mike's spirit.

## Stanley Hotel

***Estes Park, Colorado***

If Estes Park's Stanley Hotel sounds somewhat familiar, you may recall its connection with Stephen King's *The Shining*. The famous author was so impressed by his stay at the hotel (we're told he stayed in room 217) that he was inspired to write a book.

The 138-room, 1909 resort hotel is reportedly haunted. Its fourth floor is said to house a veritable playground of detached souls, complete with eerie sounds of invisible children scampering across the floor.

Realizing that this ghoulish situation might pose a liability, hotel management took a proactive approach. Rather than run from their haunted past, hotel owners ran headlong toward it.

The hotel now offers a historic ghost tour that visits the hotel's most haunted rooms and places. Place this one in the "if you can't beat 'em, join 'em" file.

## Jackalope Capital of the World

***Douglas, Wyoming***

Western towns have made some grandiose claims over the years, but declaring oneself the "Jackalope Capital of the World" is not to be taken lightly. First off, no one seems 100 percent sure whether jackalopes (deer and/or antelope crossbred with a jackrabbit) really exist. Scientists say such a species is as probable as $1 gasoline, but others aren't quite as certain.

Nevertheless, the town of Douglas sure appears to be a worthy contender in jackalope supremacy. Why? Because they say so, that's why. And they've been saying so since the *1940s!*

If that's still not enough to convince people that Douglas is the jackalope capital of the world, the town offers proof. It comes in the convincing form of an eight-foot-tall concrete statue in Douglas's downtown district, through images of the ever-elusive animal on park benches, and via pictures of the shy ones on buildings. There's even a jackalope featured on the side of Douglas's fire engines.

If still in doubt, here's the absolute clincher. Every June, Douglas plays host to "Jackalope Day." This event features such crowd pleasers as a mud volleyball tournament, motorcycle show and rally, and a greased pig run. Could the town hold such an affair if they *weren't* number one?

Then too, there's the matter of hunting licenses. Douglas issues thousands of jackalope hunting licenses each year. These hunters can only seek their prey between midnight and 2:00 A.M. each June 31 and must possess an I.Q. under 72. So there you go.

Long live the jackalope!

## World's Largest Elkhorn Arch

***Afton, Wyoming***

Elk are a pretty big deal in Wyoming, which explains Afton's arch to end all arches. Comprised of approximately 3,000 elk antlers, the arch stretches some 75 feet across four lanes of Highway 89. It weighs a whopping 15 tons.

"To duplicate this arch at today's prices, the cost would be over $300,000 for the antlers alone," proclaims an informative sign. So, who's even trying?

## World's Largest Mineral Hot Spring

***Thermopolis, Wyoming***

When you enter the town of Thermopolis (Greek for "hot city"), you're in for some thermal fun. Here, you'll derive soothing pleasure from the world's largest mineral hot spring.

Each day, the teal-colored spring issues 3.6 million gallons of water at a temperature of 127 degrees Fahrenheit. Numerous concessions make soaks in the hot mineral water available to tourists. Water temperature at these bathing sites is kept at a more reasonable 104 degrees.

It's believed that the spring possesses curative properties due to its abundance of minerals. We can't speak to that, but we will say that Thermopolis is definitely the hot spot to end all hot spots.

## Mormon Handcart Visitors' Center

***Alcova, Wyoming***

America likes its victories but *loves* its tragedies. Case in point? The Mormon Handcart story.

In July 1856, Mormon pioneers some 600 strong departed Iowa for a 1,200-mile trek to Salt Lake City. Leaving late in the season, most pulled their belongings behind them in carts. Almost immediately, trouble hit when the carts started to break. In order to lessen their load, heavy objects including blankets and winter clothes were discarded. It proved to be a deadly move. In late October, a blizzard killed 150 of the emigrants who made up the Martin party, with most perishing due to exposure.

In 1997, the Mormon Handcart Visitors' Center began to tell their story. More than 1,000 visitors arrive each day in summer to see where the tragedy occurred. Far fewer come in fall, which is not too surprising considering.

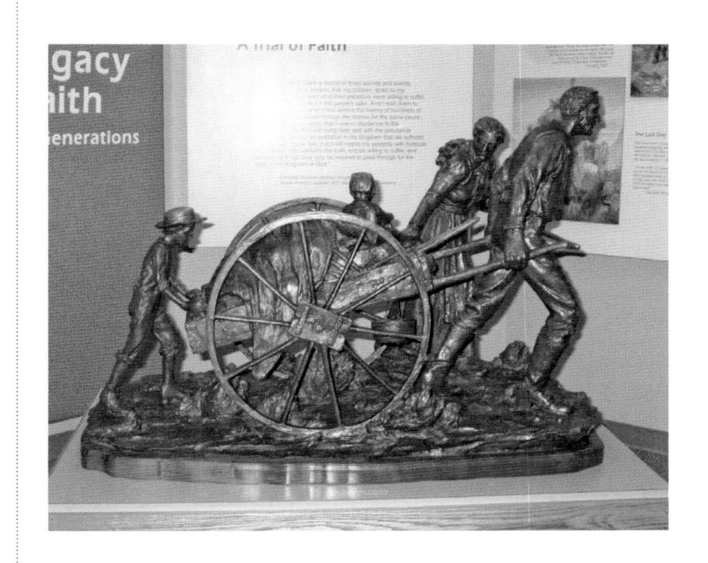

## Hell's Half Acre

***Powder River, Wyoming***

In a region brimming with geologic features, Hell's Half Acre causes even locals to take notice. Such excitement can occur when a flat plain 320 acres wide suddenly drops away to a 150-foot-deep depression for no apparent reason.

Throw in tortured rock spires painted an unnatural shade, add the requisite forbidding feel, and you have yourself an ethereal wonder.

Scientific types will spoil the fun by pointing to water and wind as the culprits responsible for this desolate hole. We prefer to think that alien bugs once walked among these rocks. From the look of things, they may still be out there.

**QUICK FACT**

The scouting team for the 1997 sci-fi movie *Starship Troopers* recognized the eerie quality of this site and quickly set up shop beside the rocks. Since they were looking to simulate an alien bug planet, the fit was ideal. All they had to do was supply the creepy crawlers and yell "Action!"

## Dinah the Pink Dinosaur

***Vernal, Utah***

Originally designed to hold a sign hawking the Dine-A-Ville Motel, the 40-foot-tall apatosaurus lost that gig when the motel fossilized. The lovable giant has now moved to the eastern end of town, where she performs chamber of commerce duty. Her new sign reads: "Vernal—Utah's Dinosaur Land." As if we couldn't tell.

## Four Corners Monument

***Utah, Arizona, Colorado, New Mexico***

Name a well-traveled American who hasn't visited the Four Corners Monument and we'll show you a life hopelessly squandered. At the geographical meeting point of Utah, Arizona, Colorado, and New Mexico, an impromptu straddling of all four states has become the savvy traveler's rite of passage.

What separates the four corners from other state meeting points is its unique corner intersection. It's also the only point in the United States that's shared by four states.

**QUICK FACT**

There's a nominal admission charge for the Four Corners Monument, but we think that's a small price to pay to be able to place each extremity in a different state at the same time.

# Bingham Canyon Mine—World's Biggest Pit

***Copperton, Utah***

This enormous copper pit mine is a fact-lover's dream. With a 17-million-ton yield thus far, it has produced more copper than any single mine in history.

Indeed, this is no ordinary mine. It is two-and-a-half miles wide and three-quarters of a mile deep.

Everything about the operation is humongous. Its electric shovels can scoop up to 98 tons in a single bite. Trucks that haul the mine's ore stand more than 20 feet tall. Even the truck driver gets to feel larger than life as he rides in a cab suspended 18 feet above terra firma.

Perhaps the best gauge of the mine's size lies in this tidbit: If you attended a rock concert here, you could bring along nine million friends!

## Hollow Mountain Gas & Grocery

***Hanksville, Utah***

You have to admire American ingenuity and pragmatism. When developers attempted to blast through a stubborn 40-foot rock to clear the way for a gas station, they abandoned the idea halfway through and hollowed out the inside instead. What they ended up with is something straight out of *The Flintstones*.

Like most service stations, Hollow Mountain Gas & Grocery sells the expected fuel and sundries, but how often does one get to pay for purchases inside a hollowed-out "mountain"? While the owners likely refer to their staff as "attendants," we think "cave dwellers" has a certain ring to it.

## Hole N" the Rock

***Moab, Utah***

Hole N" the Rock is sort of like the Hollow Mountain Gas & Grocery (previous page) on steroids. Well, apart from the fact that gasoline isn't sold here.

What is sold at Hole N" the Rock is atmosphere—oodles of it. For a nominal fee, visitors are led on a tour of the inter-mountain digs and told about its builders, Albert and Gladys Christensen.

Albert started blasting his dream home out of this natural red cliff face in the 1940s. In 1952, he and wife Gladys finally moved in. When Albert passed away in 1957, Gladys continued improving their 14-room, 5,000-square-foot cave house. She'd eventually open a gift shop and café—all the better to show the place off.

Today, a petting zoo adds to Hole N" the Rock's interesting bits, as does a not-too-faithful rendition of Franklin Delano Roosevelt carved into the rock beside the entrance. A descriptive blurb beneath declares, "Created and sculptered by artist Albert L. Christensen."

## Grafton Ghost Town

***Grafton, Utah***

Countless ghost towns exist within the Rocky Mountain region. Some are touristy affairs that smack of reproduction, others are more genuine. The one at Grafton is the real McCoy.

Grafton had its share of false starts. First settled in 1859, the town's preliminary run lasted until 1862, when a flood swept it away. After being rebuilt a mile from its original location, Grafton existed until 1866, when a rash of Indian attacks sent its 28 families scurrying. In 1868, the town was repopulated. Grafton saw dwindling population numbers from then on. By the 1930s, most people had left.

Today, a handful of people live on the town's dusty periphery, and many of its old buildings still remain. Among these are a church that was built in 1886 and a two-story private residence that is now boarded up. Nearby, Grafton's cemetery bears testament to the town's existence. Occasional tumbleweeds blowing down Grafton Road complete the desolate picture.

## Sri Sri Radha Krishna Temple

***Spanish Fork, Utah***

What could seem more out of place than a temple built in the middle of nowhere? A Hare Krishna temple built in this no-man's-land, which happens to be an acknowledged Mormon stronghold. But build it, the Krishnas certainly did. In fact, the group received a great deal of help from their Mormon brethren.

The 50-foot-tall temple juts up from its elevated plain like a proud citadel should. Exquisitely beautiful, the domed sanctuary is modeled after Kusum Sarovar, a famous palace in India.

More than 40,000 visitors tour the temple annually. Hot vegetarian meals are fed to those who hunger physically as well as spiritually, and gifts, books, and apparel are sold as souvenirs. Such is the peaceful coexistence of faiths.

## World's Largest Penguin

***Cut Bank, Montana***

Before you start in with the Tennessee Tuxedo cracks, understand that this abnormally big bird has likely heard them all by now. Besides, at 27 feet tall and some 10,000 pounds, you wouldn't want to push this guy's buttons.

Strike that. Actually you *do* want to push this seabird's buttons, at least the rather prominent one that starts him talking. So, what does he say? The tuxedoed one merely echoes the slogan painted at his base: "Welcome to Cut Bank," he enthusiastically warbles, "the coldest spot in the nation!"

Considering his heritage and overall size, we *have* to take his word for it.

**QUICK FACT**

Commemorating Cut Bank's status as the coldest town in the United States, the concrete penguin was built in 1989. It stands in front of the Glacier Gateway Inn, a furniture shop turned hotel.

## Radon Health Mines

***Basin, Montana***

In a nod to holistic treatments of the atomic age, we present the radon "health" mines of Basin, Montana. While countless companies exist solely to rid basements of dangerous radioactive radon gas, visitors to the health mines *voluntarily* expose themselves to it. Why?

Some believe that exposure to the gas can prove fruitful, particularly in the treatment of such ailments as arthritis and asthma. Each year, hundreds of people come to innocuously named places such as the Earth Angel and Sunshine Health Mines to take the cure by simply hanging around for a week or two. Others actually ingest radioactive water tainted by radon in hopes of improving their health.

Radon levels in the mines reach 175 times the federal safety standard for houses, yet the people keep on coming. Perhaps they've read a report submitted by the British Journal of Rheumatology that concludes, "This component of rehabilitative intervention can induce beneficial long-term effects." Who knew? Still, we recommend against trying this at home!

## Our Lady of the Rockies

***Butte, Montana***

Our Lady of the Rockies stands 90 feet tall and is precariously perched more than 8,500 feet up on the Continental Divide, offering an unobstructed view of some 100 miles.

Completed in 1985, the statue pays homage to women everywhere and features a memorial wall consisting of the names of 13,000 who have come before. According to David Adickes, noted sculptor of the enormous Sam Houston statue in Texas, the steel-framed lady was created to boost the town's spirits when its copper mines were shut down.

Visitors can enter the statue and peer down upon Butte, far below. For many, this is a religious experience all by itself.

## Idaho Potato Museum

***Blackfoot, Idaho***

Located in a state famous for its spuds, the Idaho Potato Museum features the World's Largest (artificial) Baked Potato as well as the World's Largest Potato Chip (it's edible but well-guarded).

From there, the display launches into all things potato, educating as it entertains. For instance, did you know that potatoes are comprised of 80 percent water and 20 percent solids? Or that french fries were introduced to America by Thomas Jefferson? Neither did we, but the Potato Museum changed all that.

**QUICK FACT**

An outdoor sign proclaims, "We Give Taters to Out-of-staters." And it's true. Visitors receive a free box of hash browns with each paid adult admission.

## Dog Bark Park Inn

***Cottonwood, Idaho***

Inside what may be the world's largest beagle, dog-tired guests spend luxurious hours dogging it. Confused? No need. The beagle in question is actually the Dog Bark Park Inn, a.k.a. "Sweet Willy"—a two-story rental unit fashioned after the popular breed. Guests are generally dog-crazy types caught up by the wonder of it all.

The inn is run by a husband-and-wife team who double as chainsaw carvers. In addition to hosting duties, the artists create doggie carvings for most popular breeds. Since the team is constantly beleaguered with questions about Sweet Willy, they've thoughtfully produced a souvenir book that tells his story from snout to tail. It's just the thing should you wish to "put on the dog" when you return home.

Ruff! Ruff!

## World's Largest Captive Geyser

***Soda Springs, Idaho***

Who would have thought that a geyser more reliable than Old Faithful existed? This one spews every hour on the hour, but there is a catch. It's regulated by humans. Still, as the World's Largest Captive Geyser, it's worth a visit.

The gushing, 100-foot-high waterspout was discovered in 1937 when a driller accidentally penetrated an underground chamber. Once the geyser sprang forth, it simply wouldn't stop erupting. Soon, enterprising types interested in tourism found a way to cap it.

Today, the water feature goes off without a hitch unless high winds preclude its release. A visitor's center explains the science behind the big gusher. Ready, set, blow!

QUICK FACT
The Caves Trail takes visitors on a winding path that leads to four different caves.

## Craters of the Moon

***Arco, Idaho***

In Idaho there's a landmass so unusual, *Apollo 14* astronauts used it to prepare for their moon mission. In reality, the craters found at Craters of the Moon National Monument are of the volcanic variety, not the result of errant meteor strikes like those found on the moon. Still, their resemblance to lunar pockmarks is almost uncanny.

Comprised of cinder cones, lava tubes, and several types of lava flows, the 60-mile-wide plain is the result of 15,000 years of volcanic activity. A seven-mile loop road takes visitors past the park's most notable volcanic features, and foot trails lead to the rest.

QUICK FACT
The cave is 1,000 feet long and is a constant 50 degrees in both summer and winter. Guided tours are available.

## Shoshone Ice Caves

***Shoshone, Idaho***

This natural wonder is indeed amazing and unusual. You'll find ice here in the middle of summer! A wooden bridge leads through the cave to a natural dead-end wall where the ice is extra thick. This is the big payoff —a sizable conglomeration of out-of-season ice.

## The Miner's Hat

***Kellogg, Idaho***

The onetime mining hotbed of the Silver Valley is a natural home for this structure, shaped like a miner's hat with a carbide lamp, at the foot of mountains once scoured for silver and gold. Originally a drive-in restaurant, the building has housed the offices of Miner's Hat Realty since the 1960s.

SIXTH ST
STOP
WEIGHT
LIMIT
10 TONS

As the most geographically diverse area in America, the Pacific landscape features an ocean, deserts, islands, mountains, and areas that split the difference among all of the above. Such differences beget other differences. Sometimes these are ordinary, sometimes extraordinary, but all add up to a region brimming with unique features.

Bearing this out, the Winchester Mystery House in San Jose, California, contains more unusual bits under one roof than are found in most *states*. If Fido wants to get in on the act, the World's Ugliest Dog Competition in Petaluma, California, provides a kooky outlet for canine companions.

The Pacific region even features a festival (the Brides of March) that mocks weddings. Good gracious, is nothing sacred? Thankfully, not in *this* amazing and unusual land!

Fabulously funky museums, folk-art extravaganzas, and a "Magical Circle" round out the Pacific's nutty repertoire. And you thought only Hollywood was strange?

*Raymond Wildlife-Heritage Sculptures Corridor, Raymond, Washington*

## Prehistoric Gardens

***Gold Beach, Oregon***

Prehistoric Gardens, the life work of Earnie Nelson, features 23 life-size prehistoric animal sculptures going about their daily lives within a soupy, natural rain forest.

Each steel and mortar replica was designed to be as scientifically correct as possible, but we could still detect a twinkle in the eye of even the most fearful specimens.

While this is no Jurassic Park (thank goodness!), the rain forest setting provides the correct backdrop to approximate the prehistoric age. Explanatory boards label each specimen and offer information about their imposing existence. If you ever wish to feel small, this is the place to visit.

## The Funny Farm

***Bend, Oregon***

The official Web site explains the Funny Farm like this: "It's a big yard art piece. It's an antique store. It's a junk store! It's a park and playground. No, it's an animal shelter isn't it? I thought it was a costume shop. Doesn't it have something to do with *The Wizard of Oz*? Who's right? They all are. More or less...."

This, better than most ads, sums up the Funny Farm. Simply put, the Funny Farm started as a second-hand store and continued to morph from there. A yard sale gave way to a bowling ball garden, which begat a vintage clothing department, which led to costume rentals. Eventually, such animals as pigs, chickens, cats, ducks, donkeys, turkeys, goats, sheep, and llamas joined the eclectic menagerie. There's even a yellow brick road leading to *Wizard of Oz* collectibles. This bit keeps people guessing while also helping to fill the coffers.

If you still don't know quite what to make of this place, rest easy, neither do we. A slogan gets to the heart of the matter. "Off Center of the Universe," reads the sign. *Way* off, we'd say.

**QUICK FACT**

Originally named "Buffet Flat," the Funny Farm was established in 1977 by owners Gene Carsey and Mike Craven.

## Perris Valley Indoor Skydiving

***Perris, California***

Despite a title that suggests pure fantasy, the Perris Valley Indoor Skydiving attraction is indeed an actual skydiving experience that is located *indoors*. How is it done?

A bank of 200-horsepower fans blows a column of air straight up a 40-foot-tall tunnel. "Flyers" with varying levels of training enter this 150-mile-per-hour environment and begin soaring.

Built to approximate the sensation of freefall, this skydiving tunnel attracts thrill seekers, who line up to take their individual turns. When it comes to skydiving, they say the sky's the limit. In this case, you might want to duck at 40 feet. Ouch!

**QUICK FACT**

Capture your flight on film! Perris Valley staff can record your flight session for posterity.

## The Brides of March

***San Francisco, California***

This annual March event aligns with the famous quip, "Take my wife, PLEASE!" as it has some fun with America's most sacred institution.

Designed to lampoon America's commercial wedding culture, the event was born in 1999 through the genius of a member of San Francisco's Cacophony Society.

The premise is quite simple. Procure a used wedding dress, put it on, and join event-goers in a bar-to-bar slosh through San Francisco. Photo opportunities, visits to jewelry stores, and mock weddings round out the special day.

## Salvation Mountain

***Niland, California***

Leonard Knight loves God, and he loves all of humankind. To underscore his feelings, the artist created a 50-foot-tall masterpiece on a barren hillside.

Festooned upon a layer of adobe clay, Knight's "canvas" includes paintings of biblical scripture, waterfalls, bluebirds, trees, flowers, and other colorful objects. A large heart situated in the middle of the piece drives the main message home.

Knight adores visitors but eschews cash contributions. He's far more interested in donations of labor and acrylic paint. Although Knight's magnum opus has been created on state land, a 2002 ruling named it a national treasure.

For the past 20 years, Knight has lived in a "house" built on the back of his two-ton 1939 Chevrolet truck, which is elaborately decorated to match the mountain he created. He has no modern amenities and chooses to rise and rest with the sun.

## Kinetic Sculpture Race

***Ventura, California***

"Where Art and Engineering Collide," reads the tagline. If this sounds perplexing, understand that this fun-filled, three-day endurance race, alternately known as the "Triathlon of the Art World," consists of funky sculptures powered solely by humans. Further challenge lies in the fact that the race traverses pavement, mud, sand, and water.

The offshoot of a 1969 tricycle race, the Kinetic Sculpture Race features homemade contraptions that use engineering to transform human energy into motive force.

Contestants are openly encouraged to cheat (yeah!) as they strive to attain the number one spot.

The race started when local sculptor Hobart Brown "improved" the look of his son's tricycle by adding extra wheels and ornamentation. Jack Mays then challenged him to a race down the street, and the two competitors, along with about a dozen other machines, raced for the first time. Neither Hobart Brown nor Mays won, however. The first winner of the Kinetic Sculpture Race was Bob Brown, whose sculpture was a smoke-emitting turtle that laid eggs.

## Burlingame Museum Of Pez Memorabilia

***Burlingame, California***

Show us a human being who hasn't heard of Pez candy, and we'll show you a life unfulfilled. Who could resist the quirky little rectangular candies that eject straight into one's hand from the equally quirky and now infamous Pez dispenser?

Gary Doss, owner of the Burlingame Museum of Pez Memorabilia, apparently lives a full life. His display of Pez and related items is nothing short of astounding. In fact, Doss showcases more than 500 characters in his Pez dispenser collection and offers many others for sale.

Opened in 1995, the museum includes such cartoon favorites as Mickey Mouse, Tweety, and Bugs Bunny, but branches out to encompass more grown-up offerings such as Uncle Sam, a wounded soldier, and a flight attendant.

The first dispensers, utilitarian in design, appeared around 1950. By 1952, cartoon heads and fruit-flavored candies had made the scene. The rest, as they say, is Pez history.

The popularity of the dispensers has turned them into highly collectible items. As proof, Doss's collection features a Mr. Potato Head knockoff that, due to its small parts, was deemed a hazard to children in 1973 and yanked from store shelves. The dispenser's current value? At least $5,000. How sweet it is!

**QUICK FACT**

Pez candy was originally introduced in Austria in 1927. The name "Pez" comes from the German word for peppermint (*pfefferminz*). Surprisingly, Pez peppermint candy was originally marketed as an adult mint to aid smokers trying to kick the habit. Who knew?

The museum is the site of the world's largest candy dispenser, as decreed by *Guinness World Records* in March 2007. Based on the design for a retired "Snowman B" (1986–2001) Pez dispenser, this giant is seven feet, ten inches tall, and weighs 85 pounds. It spits out a clear plastic capsule that can hold 6,480 Pez candies or a standard-size Pez dispenser.

## Grandma Prisbrey's Bottle Village

***Simi Valley, California***

Apparently, Grandma Tressa Prisbrey (1896–1988) hit the bottle pretty hard. At the age of 60, the intrepid woman began building bottle houses. By the time she finished in the 1980s, 33 full bottle-based structures had been completed.

Her first bottle house acted as an enclosure for her pencil collection (she had more than 10,000 pencils); her second housed a doll collection.

More than one million bottles were used to construct the village, and the mindset behind it is quite refreshing. "Anyone can do anything with a million dollars," said Prisbrey, "but it takes more than money to make something out of nothing." Indeed.

Tressa Prisbrey's life was not easy. She married her first husband when she was 15; he was 52. She had seven children by him, six of whom died. During her lifetime, death also struck her two husbands, a fiancé, and all but one of her siblings. To Prisbrey, the Bottle Village was her physical means of creating something delightful out of discard and sorrow. This is reflected in the many references to maternity and sympathetic magic, such as dolls, child-size buildings, wishing wells, and religious structures.

## Great Statues of Auburn

***Auburn, California***

While lesser street artists build their statues from delicate materials, dentist Ken Fox, the artist responsible for the Great Statues of Auburn, constructs his from solid concrete. And he likes to build BIG—a fact evidenced by the 35- to 40-foot height of his figures.

Fox began building his statues in the 1960s, a time when political statements were almost a given. His 22-foot *Chinese Coolie,* built in 1972, depicts an Asian laborer pushing a wheelbarrow. It's more than a little controversial. On the other end of the spectrum, Fox's *Coal Miner* appeals directly to the mainstream in this gold-rush territory. In fact, it was originally commissioned by the town.

The artist's statues are distributed throughout Auburn, but his most risqué works stand beside his dental office. *Freedom of Prayer* features a naked young woman with her arms projected skyward. For certain patients about to undergo root canal, this could prove more effective than Novocain.

QUICK FACT

When Fox first began raising his statues, he had quite a bit of opposition from the town. They even rerouted school buses to keep the children from seeing the contentious sculptures. But the town eventually warmed up to his creations.

## Gilroy Gardens

***Gilroy, California***

If not for one very specific area, Gilroy Gardens would be interchangeable with almost any themed amusement park. However, the *gardens* at Gilroy Gardens set it far, far apart.

The most outstanding items found among the enterprise's six gardens are its Circus Trees. These *arborsculptures* (trees shaped by grafting, bending, and pruning) differ from conventional trees much the way a Salvador Dalí painting differs from a static photograph.

Two of the park's more famous offerings are the "Basket Tree," a tree shaped like—you guessed it—a basket *(right)*, and the "Four-Legged Giant," an otherworldly tree with four separate trunks that merge into one.

Seventeen additional Circus Trees will further confound visitors' senses. Luckily, a wealth of standard garden features offset the grouping. These help viewers maintain a foothold in reality. And then, last but not least, there are the thrill rides. Whoopee!

## Desert Christ Park

***Yucca Valley, California***

Is Desert Christ Park a theme park for the faithful? Yes and no. While the park surely draws its share of believers, the 35 alabaster figures glistening in the hot, desert sun also snare the eyes of the uncommitted.

Sculptor Antone Martin created his figures and scenes in the 1950s. Constructed in concrete and painted a striking white color, the creations contrast starkly with the muted desert tones in which they're set.

A depiction of the Last Supper stands beside apostles in contemplation. The Tomb of Christ and the Garden of Gethsemane also make an appearance, as does the Sermon on the Mount.

**QUICK FACT**

Don't just capture a picture of the Last Supper, join it! The bas-relief has a convenient window (next to Jesus, of course) that allows you to enter the photo op.

## Forestiere Underground Gardens

***Fresno, California***

Baldasare Forestiere can best be described as a modern-day mole man. To escape the unrelenting heat of the San Joaquin Valley, Forestiere started boring underground in the early 1900s. Some 40 years later, he had created a subterranean complex of caverns, grottoes, and garden courts that was as pretty as it was surreal.

Since Forestiere's death in 1946, the 90 rooms that constitute the underground gardens have been operated as a museum. Today's visitor walks through a land of Roman arches, columns, and domes that provide a striking backdrop for a vast assortment of plants and trees. These include black fig, tangerine, persimmon, avocado, grapefruit, orange, mulberry, and more. Some trees are planted as deep as 22 feet below ground level. They stand as a living testament to the "mole man's" tenacity and fortitude.

**QUICK FACT**

Forestiere created his subterranean gardens by hand and with no blueprints. He based them on the "visions stored in [his] mind." He continued to extend and shape the complex throughout his life.

PLEASE
KEEP
OFF

## World's Ugliest Dog Competition

***Petaluma, California***

When does the crack "get a load of that ugly mug!" symbolize something positive? When you own a mongrel that's been entered in the World's Ugliest Dog Competition.

The contest, part of the annual Sonoma-Marin Fair, is open to any breed of dog that possesses uncommon repulsiveness. Aside from the prestige of being named the "World's Ugliest Dog," the animal's owner stands to pull in a cool $1,000 cash prize if they win.

In 2008, the top spot was nabbed by "Gus," a Chinese-crested Chihuahua with a face only a mama canine could love. It helped that Gus was completely hairless and was missing both a leg and an eye. Ugly canine champions... they're a different breed.

## Living Memorial Sculpture Garden

***Siskiyou County, California***

The Living Memorial Sculpture Garden is the antithesis of most feel-good folk-art displays. Designed to enlighten people to the plight of war and the warriors affected by such confrontations, the memorial tells a stark tale of futility as it honors those that have passed before.

Created by artist Dennis Smith, each sculpture tells a specific story. *The Refugees* looks at those souls uprooted, transplanted, and jostled about by the ever-fickle demands of war. "This type of thing happens a lot," explains Smith. "It is one of the side effects of war."

The POW-MIA *Cage* depicts a prisoner-of-war cell that speaks to the horrors of such confinement. "This statue is for all those who have been wrongfully locked up. Imagine confinement, mosquitoes, leeches,

*The Korean War Veterans Monument*

rats, rotten rice, rotten fish, abusive guards, and little chance of survival. Hope is reaching for the will to hang on!"

*Those Left Behind* features a survivor, arms outstretched in defeat, symbolically questioning what comes next. "Who can repay those who have lost loved ones in combat?" asks the artist. "What on this earth can compensate for the loss of life?"

## Galco's Soda Pop Stop

***Los Angeles, California***

John Nese has a thing for carbonation. After a prolonged period of underwhelming business at his Italian deli, Nese decided to carry soda, soda, and more soda.

Since this occurred in 1990 and the businessman's doors still remain open, it appears that Nese's gamble paid off. And why not? Everyone seems to enjoy a refreshing soda now and then, and Nese carries varieties of the bubbly liquid that defy the imagination.

If you're looking for *real* Coke (made with real sugar as opposed to high-fructose corn syrup), he's got it. Turns out the sweet concoction is bottled in Mexico by independent types with an obvious "sweet tooth."

If you fancy a sip of rose-flavored soda (and who doesn't?), Nese has that base covered as well. Marketed as Nuky Rose Soda, the Florida-made beverage is actually prepared from crushed rose petals. Slurp!

From Red Ribbon Cherry Supreme, a soda colored neon-pink, to Special Espresso Coffee Soda, a drink that uncannily resembles mud, Galco's Soda Pop Stop carries 450 different varieties of pop that run the gamut from sweet to oh-so-sweet. Could one of these smile-makers have your name on it?

## Queen Califia's Magical Circle

***Escondido, California***

This colorful sculpture garden, created by noted French artist Niki De Saint Phalle (1930–2002), consists of nine large-scale sculptures painted in a vibrant mosaic of shades.

Named for the legendary Amazon Queen, the Magical Circle includes an 11-foot-tall version of Queen Califia holding court beside a 13-foot-tall eagle. These in turn flank other sculptures, a maze entryway, native shrubs, and contemplative integrated benches.

Encircling the garden is a 400-foot undulating wall featuring playful serpents that seem ready to strike.

Billed as "the last major international project created by Niki De Saint Phalle," Queen Califia's Magical Circle is as captivating as it is confusing. Art done right is like that sometimes.

**QUICK FACT**

The sculptures feature mosaic adornments that include such materials as stone and glass.

QUICK FACT
The house originally had seven stories, but due to an earthquake in 1906, it currently has only four.

## Winchester Mystery House

***San Jose, California***

Who hasn't heard of the Winchester Mystery House? With staircases that lead to nowhere and excess of every sort, this exercise in eccentricity has become world-famous.

Legend holds that Sarah Winchester, widow of gun magnate William Wirt Winchester, was told by a psychic medium that a curse had been laid upon her. The seer explained that the curse traced back to lives cut short by the famous guns, and that Winchester should "build a home for [herself] and for the spirits who have fallen from this terrible weapon, too." Winchester was then told that she could never stop building the house. "If you continue building, you will live," said the medium. "Stop and you will die."

No one knows for sure if this actually occurred. What makes it plausible is the fact that Sarah Winchester employed a team of workers for a period of 38 years to build her home. During that time, the Victorian mansion grew to contain 160 rooms, 13 bathrooms, 47 fireplaces, 6 kitchens, 40 staircases (including a circular staircase to nowhere and stairs that mysteriously rise to a ceiling), and 10,000 window panes. Workers were in a constant state of flux, never knowing what design change would come next, or when it did, what it would entail.

Winchester died in 1922, at which point all work on the house immediately ceased. Workers were reportedly so relieved when they learned of Winchester's passing that they walked off the job, leaving protruding half-driven nails as tangible evidence of their disgust. If in fact the eccentric widow had believed the medium's words, her 38-year odyssey had been for naught.

## Watts Towers

### *Los Angeles, California*

In the annals of American folk art, few endeavors have drawn as much attention as the Watts Towers. The tall sculptural pieces, located in the economically depressed community of Watts, continue to elicit responses both positive and negative. At one point, detractors threatened to topple the tall towers, taking one man's personal creativity and art of self-expression down for the count.

In 1921, Italian immigrant Sabato "Simon" Rodia (1879–1965) had a date with artistic destiny. At his home in the Watts section of Los Angeles, the laborer dreamt of "doing something big." To accomplish the task, he gathered whatever materials he could find and started to build. Along the way, Rodia himself admitted he had little idea what would eventually materialize. Thirty years later, the folk artist would know for sure.

Using steel pipes and rods, mortar and wire mesh, Rodia built a virtual city on his tiny, one-third acre lot. Performing the task completely alone, Rodia's artistic offering featured tall towers (two approach 100 feet in height), plazas, fountains, walkways, and a gazebo. To offset their starkness, many of his works featured eye-catching shards of glass, bits of shiny porcelain, and tile. In 1954, Rodia declared his work *Nuestro Pueblo* (Spanish for "our town") and stepped aside. His masterpiece was complete.

Rodia moved from Watts in 1955, and a downward spiral of vandalism and disrepair turned many against his creation. Eventually, the city of Los Angeles declared the towers "an unauthorized public hazard" and scheduled a test of their structural integrity. If the towers could withstand a 10,000-pound stress test, the equivalent of a 76-mile-per-hour windstorm, they would be spared.

On October 10, 1959, the test commenced. A crowd of 1,000 supporters drew sighs of relief when the towers held firm. Later that year, the towers were opened to the public for a fifty-cent charge. Things were looking up. Literally.

Today, the Watts Towers stand as symbols of survival and self-expression. They have garnered enough popularity to earn a spot on the National Register of Historic Places, a feat not often awarded to folk art. If "doing something big" was Rodia's principal goal, it's a safe bet to say he succeeded. Defiant, hulking towers stand as proof.

## World's Largest Artichoke

***Castroville, California***

Down the coast a bit from San Francisco, Castroville is the "Artichoke Center of the World," thanks to its famous Green Globe 'chokes and a $50-million local industry. The city pays homage to this distinction with a 20-foot-tall steel vegetable and an annual Artichoke Festival, which named Norma Jean Baker (a.k.a. Marilyn Monroe) its inaugural Artichoke Queen in 1947.

## Gehrke's Windmill Garden

***Electric City, Washington***

If you're going to build yourself a windmill garden, it seems right and proper that it be erected in Electric City. After all, a windmill produces electricity—and Electric City, with its close proximity to the Grand Coulee Dam, seems to be the kingpin of current flow.

Despite their powerful implications, the windmills were actually built for decoration. Emile Gehrke (1884–1979) originally constructed the "wind spinners" in his backyard, but after his death many of his whimsical works were moved to a fenced-in display along a main road.

Here, visitors will find windmills designed like kettles, plates, funnels, bicycle wheels, spoons, pots and pans, and hard hats. Gehrke's presence looms large over his creations, which is none too surprising since their relationship was written on the wind.

## Milk Carton Derby

***Seattle, Washington***

Got milk? If so, you may wish to save your milk carton and at least 49 others. Only then can you enter Seattle's Milk Carton Derby.

Kicking off Seattle's Seafair celebration for better than three decades, the Derby pits ordinary citizens against corporate and military teams. The object? Make it across 1,200 feet of water in a human-powered craft built from a minimum of 50 half-gallon milk cartons.

Awards are presented in a number of categories, but the number one objective appears to be basic survival. Since a milk carton only supports four pounds of weight, there are more than a few *Titanic* incidents. Bottoms up!

## Fremont Troll

***Seattle, Washington***

Do you remember the childhood fairy tale that spoke of a troll that lived beneath a bridge? If you do, and if you're haunted by such a frightening prospect (we most certainly *are*) don't go anywhere near Seattle's Aurora Bridge. A hideous beast dwells beneath it.

The troll "sculpture" stands 18 feet tall, with a head at least half that high, and can scare a small child (and certain writers) out of a year's growth.

While it's officially said to have been sculpted by four area artists in 1990, we're not so sure. The evil gnome clutches a Volkswagen Beetle in one grimy paw. Our guess is he snatched it from the roadway above!

Some foolhardy types take their chances and clamber on top of the beast. That's a bit too risky for us.

**QUICK FACT**

Once upon a time the troll's Volkswagen contained Elvis memorabilia. This time capsule was removed after the car was vandalized. Its California license plate was also stolen during the incident.

## RichArt's Ruins

***Centralia, Washington***

Factually speaking, RichArt's Ruins is a conglomeration of trash that artist Richard Tracy has assembled. The piece consists of discarded metal pieces, chunks of Styrofoam, lightbulbs, plastic balls, and countless other items—all placed in a happenstance way along multiple "walls" throughout the complex.

From certain angles, RichArt's Ruins looks precisely like a mass of junk stuck together. From others, artistic possibilities and even small triumphs materialize. The latter is enough to keep visitors walking along to see what they'll uncover next. Perhaps this has been RichArt's intent all along?

## Fremont Rocket

***Seattle, Washington***

Erected in 1994, this genuine 1950s rocket once graced a surplus shop in Belltown. Now it stands poised for moon shots. Well, sort of.

Bedecked in snazzy metalwork, neon lights, and shiny paint, the Fremont Rocket stands before a colorful mural of clouds and distant galaxies. At regular intervals, plumes of vapor issue through its nozzles, suggesting an imminent launch.

Since it's moored to the corner of the Ah Nuts Junk Shop, the rocket is not likely to escape Earth any time soon. Still, the dreamers among us shall not be deterred.

5, 4, 3, 2, 1 . . . blast off!

**QUICK FACT**

The Rocket boasts the Fremont crest and motto "De Libertas Quirkas" on its body, which means "Freedom to be Peculiar."

## Lenin Statue

***Seattle, Washington***

What can an ultra-progressive, artistic community such as Fremont add to their enclave that might have a hope of "pushing buttons"? The world's largest Lenin statue, of course.

If your history is up to snuff, you'll recall that former Soviet Union leader Vladimir Lenin (1870–1924) was the poster boy for communism, a regime that freedom-loving Americans have had more than a few problems with throughout the years. Why then should good Washingtonians display a statue of him? Simple. Because as members of a free nation, they still *can*.

The 16-foot-tall bronze statue originally hails from Poprad, Slovakia (the former Czechoslovakia), where it was erected in 1988. When the Soviet regime went down for the count in 1989, the statue was unceremoniously tossed into a Poprad dumpsite. Rescued by American Lewis Carpenter, it was shipped to its new home in Seattle.

The statue depicts Lenin marching with a determined gait, on his way to impending revolution. The contrast of the immense communist figure standing beside thriving capitalist stores is pronounced. It suggests that—for now at least—capitalism is alive and well.

## Fremont Fair Solstice Parade

***Seattle, Washington***

When budding counter-culturists and unabashed freedom lovers seek a place to "get their groove on," they head straight for Fremont's annual Solstice Parade. Since the event features just about anything that can be conjured up artistically, plus oodles of self-expression displayed in its many, varied forms, the procession ranks as one of the most eclectic in the world.

Detractors speak of the parade's crazy pop-art, antiestablishment statements, and general lunacy. Backers point to its freedom of expression, transcendence of boundaries, and philanthropic roots.

But all, and we repeat ALL, will tell you of its frequent nudity and the throng of naked bicycle riders that "crash" the event each year. It's a real showstopper and a renewable lure that continually draws in crowds.

When the first parade was held in 1989, it drew about 300 people. Twenty years later, Seattleites in the tens of thousands wait with bated breath to see what will go down next. Main moral: People love to mix.

**QUICK FACT**

Like to plan your vacations well in advance? Here are some of the future dates of the Fremont Fair Solstice Parade: June 18, 2011; June 23, 2012; and June 22, 2013.

**QUICK FACT**

The Teapot Dome is listed on the National Register of Historic Places.

## Teapot Dome gas station

***Zillah, Washington***

Built in 1922 as a comic rebuttal to the Teapot Dome oil deals—a salacious political scandal of the 1920s—this is said to be the country's oldest operating gas station. Shaped like a 15-foot-tall teapot, the building is one of the most recognizable structures along I-82 in southern Washington.

## Bob's Java Jive

### *Tacoma, Washington*

A stellar example of programmatic architecture, Bob's Java Jive is a throwback to a fun era that featured many such wondrous establishments. The fact that it still stands makes it one rare pot indeed.

Originally dubbed the Coffee Pot Restaurant when it opened in 1927, the 25-foot-tall, 30-foot-diameter coffee pot served, among other things, piping hot coffee. It operated in this capacity for a few years then morphed into a drive-through restaurant. At one point during its illustrious history, it even became a speakeasy.

In 1955, the establishment was purchased by Bob and Lylabell Radonich and rechristened Bob's Java Jive, a nighttime "hot" spot. After remorphing into a karaoke bar and then into a go-go club, the coffee pot poured its way into the new millennium, only slightly worse for all its wear.

Today, the pot has become a beloved icon and an instantly recognizable feature on the Tacoma landscape. It is still owned by the Radonich family (though Bob Radonich passed into that great percolator in the sky in 2002 at the seasoned age of 83) and currently features area rock 'n' roll bands along with strong cups of Joe.

But the main thing is that Bob's Java Jive, a chunk of artistic pop culture from a far-off time, is *still* standing. Almost inexplicably, this little-pot-that-could has weathered repeated storms of change and warmed the hearts (and bellies) of many as it has spanned the ages. For that, we should all raise our cups.

# World's Largest Frying Pan (Almost)

***Long Beach, Washington***

What was once billed as the world's largest frying pan has sadly slipped from the top shelf—and there's not a can of PAM in sight to blame it on. The fact is, this giant nine-foot, six-inch pan was simply outpanned by other towns.

The frying pan was built in 1941 for use in the town's annual Clam Festival. These days, however, the only thing cooking at the pan is a sizzling photo op.

**QUICK FACT**
From time to time, the big pan travels throughout the northwest to promote the Long Beach area.

## Hat n' Boots gas station

***Seattle, Washington***

A landmark in Seattle's Georgetown neighborhood, this massive hat and boots once housed a service station office and restrooms, respectively. After a lengthy stay on Route 99 (Route 66's sister road), the establishment shut down in 1988 and was the victim of roadside neglect. In the 1990s, a grassroots movement emerged to save it, and the city has since restored and relocated the landmark to Oxbow Park.

## World's Largest Red Wagon

***Spokane, Washington***

Located above the Spokane River in Riverfront Park, this enormous (12 feet high and 27 feet long) red Radio Flyer wagon can hold a small army of children—the maximum capacity is 300. Named The Childhood Express, the 26-ton plaything is an interactive monument to childhood: Visitors can climb up a ladder on the back and slide down the handle.

The wagon was commissioned by the Jr. League of Spokane and is the work of local artist Ken Spiering.

## Cedar Creek Treehouse

***Ashford, Washington***

Adventure seekers looking for unique digs will be hard-pressed to outdo the Cedar Creek Treehouse, located at the base of majestic Mount Rainier. From a 50-foot perch on a fragrant cedar tree, these accommodations offer a bird's-eye view of the mountain.

Built in 1982 and placed within the "arms" of a Western Red Cedar tree, the 16- by 16-foot cabin currently operates as a bed-and-breakfast.

An 80-foot suspension bridge followed by a five-story stairwell takes one up, up, up to the unique lodge. Guests who've stayed at the treehouse speak of deliciously fresh air, spiritual renewal, and a newfound sense of peace. Funny, we thought a blister or sprain might work its way into their tales.

**QUICK FACT**

Amenities at Cedar Creek include a one-hour guided tour of the area, which takes place approximately 100 feet in the sky! Guests are free to film and photograph the incredible sights.

## Waterfront Exercise Equipment

***Vashon Island, Puget Sound, Washington***

Here's one that's so silly it had to be included. Six fully functional exercise bicycles and two step machines sit overlooking Puget Sound on a land bridge connecting Vashon Island with Maury Island. How and why they are here is anyone's guess.

Could the donor be an exercise junkie looking for an on-the-fly endorphin release? Might he/she be a person who has declared war on calories? Is the exercise enthusiast a few spokes shy of a full wheel?

These earth-shattering questions may never find an answer, but that's not important. There's much peddling to do, ladies and gentlemen, so have at it!

## Raymond Wildlife-Heritage Sculptures Corridor

***Raymond, Washington***

In and around the town of Raymond, mysterious metal figures dot the landscape. Numbering some 200 pieces in all, the sculptures spice up Highway 101, State Route 6, and parts of the town and include Native Americans, loggers, bears, horses, oxen, foxes, and birds, among other things. The pieces were created by local artists, and many embody the heritage of the region. Heavily rusted and gritty after years spent in a wet climate, the statues suggest equal grit in the people and animals they depict.

**QUICK FACT**

Think the statues are so neat that you'd like one for yourself? Replicas are available for purchase through the Raymond Chamber of Commerce.

## Hobo Inn

***Elbe, Washington***

Near the foot of majestic Mount Rainier, the Hobo Inn is the place to bed down for the night for an experience that melds creature comforts with the hobo lifestyle. The proprietors have converted about a half-dozen vintage cabooses into motel rooms (scarf on a stick not included). The oldest of the rail cars dates to 1916.

**QUICK FACT**

If you're a hobo that likes the finer things in life, never fear: The Hobo Inn features a room with a private whirlpool.

## Anchorage Light Speed Planet Walk

***Anchorage, Alaska***

The Anchorage Light Speed Planet Walk has people traveling faster than they ever thought humanly possible.

So what is it? Basically it's a scale model built to human dimensions and spread throughout the city. Walking from the sun to the moon takes approximately eight minutes—the time it takes a light beam to cover the distance across the cosmos.

For math aficionados, this means each step equals the distance that light travels in one second, or 186,000 miles. And you thought drag-racers were fast.

Eli Menaker, a 2004 Service High School graduate, devised the model as a way for people to wrap their minds around the enormous size of our solar system. Each planet is represented at a different location around the city, and a special indoor solar system exhibit lies on the path to Mercury. It's a small *universe*, after all.

While Alaska is by far America's largest state, its 1867 acquisition by Secretary of State William H. Seward was originally considered a blunder. Critics attacked the secretary for spending 7.2 million dollars on what they referred to as "Seward's Icebox" or, alternately, "Seward's Folly."

A century later when up from the ground came a bubbling crude (oil, that is), Seward's "folly" proved to be anything but. The Trans-Alaska Pipeline has pumped more than 15 billion barrels of oil since it went online in June 1977. At present market rates, that's a phenomenal return on investment. Seems to us "Dollar Bill" got it exactly right.

## World's Largest Maze

***Oahu, Hawaii***

Nothing says "Hawaii" like the pineapple. And nothing says "pineapple" like the Dole Plantation in Hawaii. But if the pineapple doesn't get your juices flowing, we're sure that this will: The Dole Plantation is home to the World's Largest Maze. In 2001, *Guinness World Records* put its stamp of approval on the "world's largest" claim. And if it's good enough for *Guinness,* it's good enough for us!

**QUICK FACT**

The Pineapple Garden Maze is made of more than 11,000 varieties of Hawaiian plants and covers three acres of land. The path through the maze is 3.11 miles, so you'll want to be sure to wear your walking shoes. We think this sounds like an attraction we could really get "lost" in!

# INDEX

## n



## O



## P



## Q



## R



## S



## T



## U



## V

## W



## Y

# GEOGRAPHICAL APPENDIX